# SOCIAL CLASS ON CAMPUS

# Social Class on Campus

## Theories and Manifestations

WILL BARRATT

1996–2011 15TH ANNIVERSARY

Stylus

PUBLISHING, LLC.

STERLING, VIRGINIA

Published by Stylus Publishing, LLC
22883 Quicksilver Drive
Sterling, Virginia 20166-2102

Library of Congress Cataloging-in-Publication Data
Barratt, Will, 1950-
Social class on campus : theories and manifestations /
Will Barratt.—1st ed.
    p.   cm.
Includes bibliographical references and index.
ISBN 978-1-57922-571-1 (cloth : alk. paper)
ISBN 978-1-57922-572-8 (pbk. : alk. paper)
ISBN 978-1-57922-573-5 (library networkable
e-edition)
ISBN 978-1-57922-574-2 (consumer e-edition)
1. Educational equalization—United States.
2. Academic achievement—United States.
3. Minorities—Education—United States.   I. Title.
LC213.2.B365   2011
306.43—dc22
                                        2010040709

13-digit ISBN: 978-1-57922-571-1 (cloth)
13-digit ISBN: 978-1-57922-572-8 (paper)
13-digit ISBN: 978-1-57922-573-5 (library networkable
e-edition)
13-digit ISBN: 978-1-57922-574-2 (consumer e-edition)

Printed in the United States of America

Bulk Purchases

Quantity discounts are available for use in
workshops and for staff development.
Call 1-800-232-0223

First Edition, 2011

10   9   8   7   6   5   4   3   2   1

# Contents

# Acknowledgments

I HAVE BEEN INTERESTED in social class for quite a while, and my movement toward this book had several critical incidents and many helping hands. I remember sitting with a faculty colleague and six master's students in the food court in New Orleans during lunch at an annual meeting of the American Counseling Association. I like to present at conferences so I asked if anyone wanted to write a presentation proposal for the conference scheduled in Anaheim the following year. Four students, Heather Burrow, Colleen Kendrick, Julie Parrott, and Kristin Tippin, said yes and we met weekly for the next few months to develop the proposal and then met again to develop the presentation. The intellectual and emotional contributions of these women to my thinking have been deep and sustaining.

The next year I looked for copresenters for a state conference and was lucky enough to find Leslie Jowarski and Amy Welch to work with. Their insights, thoughts, and contributions to my understanding of class were critical. After that, each conference presentation brought new insights, and the audience participants were willing contributors to ever more complex ways of discussing social class. I am grateful to my copresenters, Dan Stoker, Carey Treager-Huber, and Mary Springer, and everyone in attendance at each of our presentations.

Diane Cooper sought me out at a conference and said bluntly, "You have to do something with this stuff." So I started this book. I kept presenting at conferences as a way to refine and deepen the dialogue about class on campus, and I kept listening to people. Along the path I had wonderful conversations with Ken Barr, Tracy Davis, Donna Talbot, Aimee Medina, Matt Draper, Janet Weirick, and many others.

Often these conversations were an excuse for me to think out loud while talking with smart, articulate, and interesting people.

Writing is difficult for me, and I am particularly grateful for the encouragement of Sarah Burrows and John von Knorring. I am ever grateful to Fran Hatton, who took the first look at the entire manuscript and said, "This is pretty good," and then she told me all the things to fix. Throughout the text I have added references to people who have turned the right phrase at the right time, who have helped with the stories, or who have directly helped, so look for their names.

To everyone known and unknown—thanks.

# About the Author

PLACING AUTHORS IN CONTEXT is important since we all approach material from our own point of view. I am a European American college professor born in 1950. My maternal line traces to the 1600s with English immigrants who settled in New England and a paternal line of English and German immigrants who came to the United States in the 1880s. While I identify with the geographical location of my mother's family I identify with the intellectual heritage of my father's family. My paternal grandfather, the English side, went to Worcester Polytechnic Institute, became an engineer and later a vice president of human resources. My paternal grandmother, the German side, went to a women's finishing school and was a stay-at-home mom. My father had a PhD from an Ivy League school, a Stanford postdoc; was a professor of biology at an Ivy League school; and was later dean of sciences at a California state college. My mother, the New England side, was one of the last generation born on Moosebrook Farm in Massachusetts, ending a line from before U.S. independence from England. My mother went to the University of New Hampshire, got a BS in biology, and became a stay-at-home mom. She was a first-generation college student, as were her brother and sister. I am third-generation college and second-generation PhD. My sister went to a Seven Sisters college, and I went to an ACM college. My oldest child and my sister's oldest went to an Ivy League and a Seven Sisters college respectively, and our second children both went to an ACM school. I have a PhD in student development in postsecondary education from a Big Ten school, my wife has a Big Ten PhD in linguistics and is a professor of linguistics, and my sister has a Big Ten PhD in developmental psychology and is now dean of arts and sciences at a prestigious research university. Our first cousin is a physician, and we count him among the five Doctor Barratts in our lineage. This says a lot about my social class of origin and about my attributed social class. It provides some perspective on my view of social class on campus. My current felt social class is another matter.

## About the questions in this book

I am at heart a classroom teacher and a discussion facilitator. A good discussion question leads to more, better, more articulate, and more interesting questions. For me good questions have complicated answers. When I was teaching at a selective state university in Ohio I would often answer student questions with, "It depends," and then go on to explore what the answer would depend on. Students, and most of us, are looking for answers. This book is filled with lots of questions and few answers.

I find it interesting that books on multicultural anything start by warning the reader not to stereotype, and then proceed to provide stereotypes for each minority group. Phrases like "African Americans are . . ." or "Hispanics are . . ." or "German immigrants are . . ." make me angry. If you are looking for a book that will tell you what upper-class people or students in poverty are like, what their values, norms, morality, and sexual activities are, this is not the book for you. If you are looking for a book that explores the underlying concept of class and helps you understand there are differences within class as well as between classes, then this is the book for you. This is not a book about diversity. This is a book about class. Diversity is about how we can all live and work together. Class is about what separates and divides us.

The questions in this book serve as rhetorical devices and as a way for you to explore what you think about class. The questions are a way for you to figure out what the answer depends on for you.

## Yes, and . . .

There is more than one way to look at anything. The more tools we use to examine a concept, the more fully we understand the concept.

The best and most confusing way to knowledge is to simultaneously apply multiple and contradictory perspectives. Using a single explanation gives rise to the false assumption that there is only a single explanation. However, it is easy to fall into the trap of thinking that words are themselves the concept. If I point at the moon, is my finger the moon? If I explore the moon with a telescope, is it the moon in the reticule? If I land on the moon and bring back moon rocks, are those rocks the moon? "The map is not the territory; the word is not the thing," one of the precepts of general semantics, is usually attributed to Alfred Korzybski. This simple statement articulates the danger inherent in every explanation.

I took the idea of "Yes, and . . ." from Professor Jim Banning, to whom I am thankful. "Yes, and . . ." encapsulates an attitude of discourse, shunning the dismissive attitude behind "Yes, but . . ."

"Yes, and . . ." embodies the multifaceted reality of which we are all a part.

# PART ONE

# Understanding Social Class

# CHAPTER 1

## A Starting Point

### Class is more than money

SAYING THAT CLASS is about money is the same as saying that ethnicity is about skin color. Money is part of class, and skin color is part of ethnicity. One sticky idea in this book, one sound bite, is this: Social class is more than rich and poor.

Most models of class are useful in some ways and inadequate in others. The trick is to figure out which model of social class works best for what you need to do. In some situations viewing class as money may be effective. Parental income is one way to group students and parents by class. In some situations viewing class as one's occupation may be effective. Parental occupation is one efficient way to group parents and students by class. In some situations viewing class as culture may be effective. Student interests and activities are important and reflect a culture-based worldview.

### Class is personal

A second sound bite, a sticky idea that makes the perspective of this book different from that of many others, is this: Social class is personal.

Much of the literature on class comes from economics and sociology. The *Publication Manual of the American Psychological Association*

(APA, 2009) notes, "Do not attribute human characteristics to animals or to inanimate sources" (p. 69). To attribute the actions of the creation of class or the act of sustaining class to an inanimate source like society or the economy is questionable. Universities don't do anything. People do things. Economies don't do anything. People do things. Societies don't do anything. People in societies do things. The idea of an economy acting in a certain way or a society acting in a certain way is an abstract fiction, albeit a useful one. The collection of individual actions must be seen for what they are, individual actions, not abstract ideas.

## Class is an intercultural experience

Milton Bennett's (1998) model of intercultural sensitivity is a useful tool to deconstruct conversations about class. In Bennett's model people move from the lowest stage, called denial, to the defense stage to minimization to acceptance to adaption to the highest stage, called integration. While Bennett's model is about intercultural sensitivity, it applies to class quite well because one way to see class is as culture. Personal reactions to differences depend on many things, and Bennett's intercultural sensitivity model is one among many useful tools for self-examination when class comes up in conversation.

*Denial.* Someone in this stage might comment: "We really don't have class in the United States." People in the denial stage about class are unaware of the reality of class-based differences among people. These individuals are unaware of the important economic, cultural, and personal differences that relate to class.

*Defense.* Typical comments from someone in the defense stage might be: "They're poor because they don't work hard," and "Those rich snobs think they're better than the rest of us." People in the defense stage have a negative attitude about the classes above or below them. In this stage people like us (PLU) are normal, and any deviation from our personal PLU norms is seen as negative or abnormal.

*Minimization.* People in the minimization stage repeat the myth, "Well, we're all really middle class anyway," minimizing and belittling real class differences and trying to make the middle class inclusive of everyone. They see all of us as having universal values rather than values derived from a classed context. Real differences are denied in this stage, and the appropriateness of alternative norms, behaviors, and so forth is not recognized. At this stage people wish that everyone were middle class so that we would all be normal. This leads to the assumption that everyone wants, or should want, to become middle class. Asking, "Why can't we all just get along?" is another way to minimize real class differences.

Myths about class are artifacts of denial, defense, and minimization. Individuals in Bennet's (1998) stages of acceptance, adaptation, and integration see class differences for what they are and work on understanding their own cultural assumptions.

## Class is individual perception

How we see class is important. If we see class as being about money, then we will identify money problems within class and pursue money-related solutions to these problems. If we see class as external to the individual, our understanding of class, the problems we see, and the solutions we promote will reflect this idea that class is external to the individual. If we see class as internal to the individual, and this is the primary model of class used in this book, then the problems we see and the solutions we promote will reflect this individual view of class. If we see class from multiple perspectives, from a more complicated view, then our understanding of the problems of class will be richer, the problems we see will be more complete, and the solutions we promote will be more broad based. Class is money and wealth and cultural capital and prestige and educational attainment and many other things.

Social class is more than rich and poor.

## Class as a tool

Which type of screwdriver do you prefer: a Phillips head or a slot head? Most people don't know much about screws and screwdrivers and have no preference, and many people answer they prefer a Phillips head screwdriver. The right answer of course is that you prefer the screwdriver that matches the screw you need driven. We all have used the wrong tool on occasion. I recall removing a slot head screw with lobster claw pliers because the slot had been stripped out of the screw head. While I had wished the screw had a Phillips head because it is less likely to strip out a Phillips head screw, the screw head was not a Phillips head, and my wishing it so did not make it so. Using my power screwdriver, I have managed to strip out my share of Phillips head screws even when I use the right screwdriver. First, using the right tool for the job is important, and second, even with the right tool you can apply too much power or use it inappropriately. Models of social class are tools, and the tools we use should meet the needs we have.

## A word about precision

What is simple is rarely true, and what is true is rarely simple. Aristotle, writing in Book 1, Chapter 3 of *Nicomachean Ethics*, has an interesting observation on precision:

> It is the mark of an educated man [*sic*]to look for precision in each class of things just so far as the nature of the subject admits; it is evidently equally foolish to accept probable reasoning from a mathematician and to demand from a rhetorician scientific proofs. (Aristotle, trans. 1976).

The level of precision is one way to distinguish various disciplines. The social sciences work with notable levels of imprecision. Standard errors of measurement are substantial in the typical quantitative measures employed in psychology, sociology, and education. Imprecision makes for complicated interpretations. Similarly, concepts like class are inherently imprecise. The idea of a photon is based on a physical object or event. Having a physical reality of some sort creates one level of precision. The idea of class is based on the observations of large groups of people and on the observations of people within groups, and this creates an entirely different level of precision. Unlike photons, there is no physical object or event behind social class. Research on social class is fraught with the problem of precision.

## Class as identity

The contemporary United States of America has been called an identity society. We all develop a gender, ethnic, and class identity at an early age as we go through a process of identification and differentiation. Gender and ethnic identity do not change for most people, and in a society without class movement class identity does not change. However, we know that class movement, either up or down, is a fact of life for many in the United States. This dynamic class movement gives rise to the idea that we all have a social class of origin, a current felt social class, and an attributed social class, where we came from, what we think of ourselves, and what others think of us (Barratt, 2005). As first-generation students move up in social class because of their education, a mismatch between their class identities arises. It should not go without notice that this internal identity conflict can engender attendant psychological symptoms of anxiety and depression. This tripartite notion of class identity is the third sound bite, the third sticky idea in the book.

We all have a social class of origin, a current felt social class, and an attributed social class.

## Class as income and wealth

The reality of class depends on how we describe class. The simplest answer is that class is about money, and money is income for most people. There are huge disparities in Americans' earnings, and income certainly is one way to keep score. Is a trucker who makes $80,000 a year in the upper-middle class? If we use groups of 20% of the population based on family income we get five evenly sized groups, and subdivide the top 20% to create an elite class with the 5% highest income.

## FIGURE 1
### Family Income (2008)

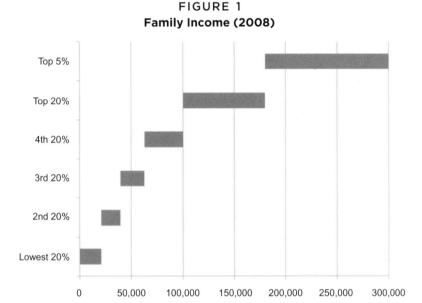

*Note:* Adapted from U.S. Census Bureau. (2008b). *Income: Households, Table H-1. Income Limits For Each Fifth and Top 5 Percent, All Races.*

Figure 1 of the income tables from the U.S. Census Bureau (2008b) shows income for these six groups in 2006 U.S. dollars.

Income is potential wealth, and wealth is accumulated economic assets. In the contemporary United States only a small percentage of the population has any wealth at all, and most of that is in home equity. Most people owe more money than they have. Mortgages, car loans, credit card debt, school loans are all balanced against home equity, savings, and retirement dollars. Class as wealth is useful when making a distinction among the wealthy, but most people have no liquid wealth like savings or investments.

## Class as capital

While Marx (1885/1948) used economic capital as one analytic tool to examine class, other authors, like Bourdieu (1986) in "The Forms of

Capital," suggested that class should also include social and cultural capital. Social capital is an interpersonal network of people who can collaborate and join their resources. Put simply by professor and author Michael Cuyjet: "It's not who you know, it's who knows you."

Cultural capital is the knowledge and skills of the prestige class. College is an opportunity to build both. Other forms of capital, such as academic capital, may be used to examine the role of class on campus. Social and cultural capital takes time and skill to build. We all start to build capital at home, and coming from a wealthy home means being economically, socially, and culturally wealthy.

## Class as education

August Hollingshead (1957, 1975) used educational attainment and occupational prestige to measure social status. Education is not evenly or randomly distributed in adults over 25 in the United States (see Figure 2) according to the U.S. Census Bureau (2008a).

We can use educational attainment to make five meaningful and unequal sized groups as shown in Figure 3.

## Class as prestige

In U.S. American culture, prestige is an obvious marker indicating the best product, service, or educational institution. The word *prestige* is used in this book instead of *status* because prestige is a higher-prestige word than status. Higher-prestige colleges are considered better colleges. Higher-prestige varieties of English are considered better English. Higher-prestige clothing, purses, and accessories are considered better. Higher-prestige beer is considered better. When higher-prestige anything is put to a test, the product, service, or educational institution is often not better quality. A student in one of my classes, Aimee Medina, coined the phrase "obviously labeled fashion" to describe large logo designs seen on consumer products, and I added the phrase "subtly labeled fashion" to reflect smaller, more discreet, and consequently

### FIGURE 2
**Percentage of U.S. Adults Over 25 at Degree Levels**

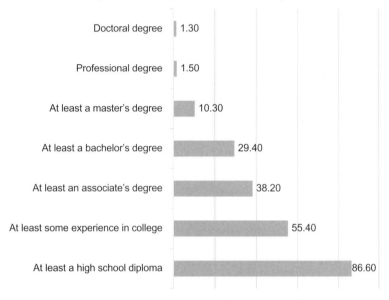

Doctoral degree | 1.30

Professional degree | 1.50

At least a master's degree | 10.30

At least a bachelor's degree | 29.40

At least an associate's degree | 38.20

At least some experience in college | 55.40

At least a high school diploma | 86.60

*Note.* Adapted from *Educational Attainment in the United States: 2008—Detailed Tables. Table 1, all races*, by U.S. Census Bureau, 2008.

### FIGURE 3
**Educational Attainment of Adults Over 25**

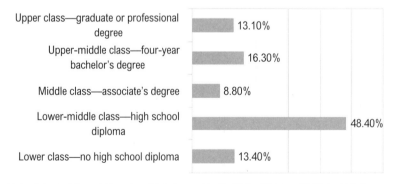

Upper class—graduate or professional degree | 13.10%

Upper-middle class—four-year bachelor's degree | 16.30%

Middle class—associate's degree | 8.80%

Lower-middle class—high school diploma | 48.40%

Lower class—no high school diploma | 13.40%

*Note.* Adapted from *Educational Attainment in the United States: 2009*, by U.S. Census Bureau, 2009.

more prestigious logos. Labeled fashions are one way to purchase prestige, and economists call items purchased for prestige *positional goods*. When education is seen as a commodity in the educational marketplace then it is possible to see some colleges as prestige luxury goods, some colleges as mass-market goods, and other colleges as big-box discount goods.

While most people think as if class were money, most people behave as if class were prestige.

## Class as occupation

In the United States, occupation is an important prestige marker. The last large-scale examination of occupational prestige was undertaken by Davis, Smith, Hodge, Nakao, and Treas (1991) and provides an overview of what Americans believe about occupation and prestige. Over 500 occupational titles were arranged in a hierarchy of prestige based on what a large sample of the U.S. population believes. While there is equal dignity in being a professor or a plumber, the prestige is different.

## Class as culture

Social class is a collection of cultures arranged in a hierarchy of prestige. Class can be seen as a collection of cultures that have shared values, rituals, beliefs, slang, and even language. When class is seen as culture, then all the tools to examine, think about, and work with culture come into play. When cultures are seen as equivalent and class is seen as culture, the inherent inequity of class is ignored. This is a bad thing.

## Class as a system

When class is seen through a systems lens, institutions like banks and schools take on a role in the re-creation and reproduction of class

(Bourdieu, 1986). These systemic class differences are reflected in all aspects of the campus, from its prestige to admissions requirements to marketing to rankings in popular media. Social class is a messy human system of connections and interconnections. Class is a self-organizing social system we all create, and our individual actions through our institutions reproduce our class system.

## Class as privilege and oppression

One of the consequences of a social hierarchy is that some people are privileged and some people are oppressed. The agents of privilege and oppression are the people in the system who cocreate that system of privilege and oppression. Oppression is not an abstract idea. The actions of a member of one group that negatively sanction the member of another group is an act of oppression. Professors are privileged every time someone uses their educational attainment (doctor) or position (professor) as a form of address.

## Class as role

Goffman (1959) wrote about the roles we play and the construction of those roles in *The Presentation of Self in Everyday Life*. When seen as a role, class takes on new dimensions appropriate to a play or film. Costuming, dialect, physical action, placement in the shot or on the stage are all part of analyzing a theater and social class role. Take the examples of costuming and dialect in a movie. It is easier to change your costume than your dialect. Physical performance in any social interaction can be read as classed behavior. Who greets whom, who touches whom, who initiates introductions are all dimensions of class.

## Social class on campus

All campuses have a majority social class, just as they have average SAT/ACT scores, a majority ethnicity, a gender ratio, a graduation rate, and even average parental income. These are all markers for the campus's social class. These are the characteristics of the majority of students. The campus physical plant reflects the campus social class environment. High-prestige campuses have more prestigious architectural and physical features than low-prestige campuses; community college architecture is mocked as "High School High" even by community college students. The campus social organization as seen in the campus organization chart, the arrangement of management structures, and the presence of support services reflects the campus's social class. The majority social class environment on campus reinforces majority students' beliefs about class and challenges everyone not in the majority.

## Campus majority social class

The simplest indicator of campus social class culture is the social class of the majority of the students. Most campuses have a majority of students whose parents went to college. Most campuses have a majority of women students. It must be noted that 50% of the students at community colleges are first-generation students whose parents have no experience on any campus. Community college student enrollment reflects the national educational attainment average. However, only 27% of students at four-year colleges are first-generation students (National Center for Education Statistics [NCES], 1998). The perpetuation of class in the educational system is a fact of life.

What is the average income of students' parents on your campus? What is the average educational attainment of the parents of the full-time students on your campus? What are the class markers of students on your campus?

## Class is more than money

The model, metaphor, and language we use for class determine how we think and feel about class and how we choose to act. Class is typically treated at the macro level. The large-scale economic trends, the large-scale social trends, and the assumptions and language used in macroeconomics and macrosociology drive how people think and feel and act about class. How we think and feel about class determines how we act about class. If class is seen as a macro-level sociological, economic, or group phenomenon then your work with class will be with groups and not with individuals. If class is seen as economic, your work with class will be economic. If class is seen as cultural, then your work with class will be about culture. Having multiple models, being multi-paradigmatic, will enable you to think about class in multiple ways and give you multiple choices for your actions.

## Class bubbles

Circles of sameness is one way to describe class bubbles, the class systems we inhabit. Unless you make an effort, most of your colleagues, friends, and family are a lot like you and reside in the same or similar class bubble. "Why are all the rich kids sitting together in the cafeteria?" Birds of a feather dine together. Your class bubble becomes your standard and affects your sense of what is normal when you compare yourself to others. If you are a third-generation student and attend a private college, that is normal for you, and you could believe it to be normal for everyone. We each create our own lives with what is familiar, and class is one of the features of our lives that drive who we spend time with and what we do and what we eat and what we drink. If you don't live in a class bubble, good for you. If you don't live in a gender, ethnic, or class bubble, great for you.

## A tale of five students: Whitney Page, Louise, Misty, Ursula, and Eleanor

The names of these five fictional women are class mnemonics for working/poverty class (Whitney Page), lower class (Louise), middle class (Misty), upper-middle class (Ursula), and elite class (Eleanor). Their stories are based on people I know and are used to illustrate salient features of class on campus. To foreground class and remove the complexity of ethnicity and gender that can make conversations of class overwhelmingly complicated, these students are all European American women. Narratives from men and from ethnic minorities are included in a later section after the stories of these five fictional characters have been used to present basic concepts. Choosing to use women as examples removes issues related to stereotypes about men. A story about Bob, a poverty/working-class man who is having difficulty adjusting to life on campus and is experiencing anxiety, can easily lead the reader to urge Bob to "man up."

These five fictional students are ethnically, cognitively, and physically similar. They look a lot alike, are about the same height, have the same north European complexion, and have brown curly hair. They each have an IQ (within a standard error of measurement) of about 130 and each has a combined SAT score (verbal plus quantitative and within a standard error of measurement) of about 1,350. They get good grades (averaging above a B plus) in school. The differences are important also. Whitney Page, Louise, Misty, and Ursula all grew up in the same midwestern state about 100 miles from each other and are similarly attractive. Eleanor grew up in New York City and is rather plain looking.

## The cast of characters: Whitney Page

Whitney Page comes from the working/poverty class. She lives in a small city whose industrial base has crumbled. She is the oldest child and has two sisters and a brother. Her father died in a car accident five years ago. Her mother, aunts, and uncles have a high school education, as do two of her grandparents. The other two grandparents quit school to work to help their families. No one in her family has had a career, but all have had a series of jobs. The media would refer to them as the working poor. Most of her relatives live within 20 miles of each other. When some financial disaster befalls the family of one of her adult relatives, the children get sent to live with cousins. None of the families are ever far from financial disaster. Her family is on food stamps and all the children get free breakfasts and lunches at school. Her mother works full-time, and the family lives in subsidized housing.

In elementary school Whitney Page's mother set up a token economy at home to teach her children about money and budgeting. When she was old enough, Whitney Page got an after-school job and gave the money to the family. Whitney Page's mother believes in the importance of education, and the children are expected to do well in school. Whitney Page is the most academically talented of the children. In middle school she enrolled in a program for students who were getting free and reduced lunches that would pay for college tuition if she maintained a B average and stayed out of trouble. She ran track for two years in high school but stopped when she got an after-school job. Back to school was always her favorite time of the year because it meant that she got two new pairs of pants. Her schools have always been below standard in measures of student achievement, even though other schools in the same district receive awards for student achievement. The teachers in her school have the least education and are among the least qualified in the district.

She has lived in a working/poverty-class bubble all her life, surrounded by people at home, at work, and at school who are culturally, socially, and financially like her. Whitney Page has low economic capital, low cultural capital, low social capital, and few social skills she could use on a college campus. Students like Whitney Page are unlikely to continue their education beyond high school and have low attendance and graduation rates at four-year colleges.

### The cast of characters: Louise

Louise comes from the lower-middle class. She lives in a small farming town that maintains traditional midwestern values. She has a younger brother. Her father is a farmer with his own corn and bean fields, and her mother works as an office assistant in town. Two of her aunts have jobs like her mother's and the other one works on the farm. Two of her uncles farm, and the third works at the grain elevator in town. Her grandfathers on both sides were farmers and are now retired. Neither parent went to college nor did her aunts, uncles, and grandparents.

Work choices are farming or a job in town. No one she knows well has a career. In high school she played volleyball, basketball, and ran track. Louise has been to Chicago and St. Louis on school trips and goes to the state capital occasionally with her family. She has worked at Dairy Queen since she was 16, and she was an active participant in 4-H. For her high school graduation trip Louise went with a large group to Disney World.

She has lived most of her life in a working-class bubble, surrounded by people ethnically, culturally, socially, and financially like her. Louise has modest economic capital, modest cultural capital, limited social capital, and limited interpersonal skills when dealing with people from an obviously higher social class. Students like Louise occasionally attend a four-year college and graduate at rates below the national average.

## The cast of characters: Misty

Misty comes from the middle class. She grew up in an upscale suburb north of a major city. She has one younger brother. Her parents are business executives who were second-generation college students. Her mother has an MBA and works in a manufacturing company. Her father has a BA in business and works in the central office of a whole-sale cleaning products company. Misty's aunts and uncles all have college educations and all have careers of some sort working for large corporations. Her grandfathers graduated from college with degrees in agriculture and went into farming. Her maternal grandmother went to college for one year and worked as an office assistant. Her paternal grandmother was a stay-at-home mom on the farm. Most of her relatives live over 250 miles away. Most of her friends are European American, and her few non-European friends have well-educated and professional parents.

Misty goes to the nearby city almost once a month but typically shops at the local upmarket mall. She has been on family vacations to New York, Chicago, Los Angeles, London, Paris and Nice, and Rome, staying in Hilton Hotels in all these cities because her father likes Hiltons and gets a discount. Misty has never worked or volunteered except for Sunday school at church. She was a Girl Scout for two years and was not involved in organized high school activities. Her parents gave her a lot of freedom as a child and gave her a car when she was 16.

Misty has lived in a middle-class bubble, surrounded by people ethnically, culturally, socially, and financially like her. She is economically advantaged, has moderate cultural capital, moderate social capital in her community, and moderate skills at building cultural capital. Misty's parents value economic capital a great deal, they devalue cultural capital, and they value social capital only in the context of getting ahead and making more money at work. Students like Misty are likely to attend and graduate from college.

### The cast of characters: Ursula

Ursula comes from the upper-middle class. She grew up in a college town where her father is a professor and her mother is a physician. She has one younger brother. Her paternal aunt is a professor. Her paternal grandfather was a professor and her paternal grandmother was a librarian; both were first-generation immigrants. Her paternal great-grandfather and maternal great-grandfather were engineers, and their wives ran their households in London, where they lived. Her maternal grandfather, a first-generation college-educated immigrant, taught himself engineering after he came to the United States and built a small manufacturing company in the ship machinery business. Her maternal grandmother worked as an executive secretary in a New York publishing house. Every one of her immediate relations has a career. Ursula lived in Budapest for a year when she was three and went to a Hungarian day care facility. She lived in Tokyo for a year when she was 13 and went to a Japanese school. At 15 she spent her summer as an exchange student in Monterrey, Mexico, living with a family and going to school. She spent her junior year of high school in Belgium as an exchange student. In high school she was in the Latin Club and was assistant director of one of the school plays.

Ursula does not live in a bubble. Her international experiences helped her understand multiple culture, gender, ethnic, and class perspectives. Ursula is economically advantaged; has a great deal of cultural capital; and has more than adequate social capital, as well as the skills to build more social capital to help her succeed on campus. Ursula's parents value cultural and social capital over economic capital. Students like Ursula are very likely to attend and graduate from college.

### The cast of characters: Eleanor

Eleanor is from the elite upper class. She lives in New York City and comes from old money—the elite wealthy who aren't employed. She is not from the working wealthy. She has one younger brother. Her father has a law degree from an Ivy League school, sits on the boards of a law firm, several hospitals, and one major corporation. Her mother has an MBA from a high-prestige university and spends her time managing the family, staff, and homes. She sits on the boards of several New York–based charities. Her academically talented aunts, uncles, cousins, and relations were all educated at highly selective universities. Those who were not academically talented attended schools like the flagship state university (TFSU). Eleanor went to private elementary day school in New York City and attended a residential private high school in New England where she rowed crew. She has traveled extensively with family and friends, much of it to fulfill social obligations with international friends.

She has lived her life in a protected social class bubble among people with wealth and has always been aware of class and wealth. Students like Eleanor are expected to attend and succeed at college.

Whitney Page's, Louise's, Misty's, Ursula's, and Eleanor's class assignment depends on how you classify class, on how you draw the boundaries between classes. If we use U.S. demographics for parental educational attainment, we get one answer. Whitney Page and Louise are in the bottom 72% because their parents don't have a college education, Misty is in the top 28% for one parent and the top 9% because one parent has an MBA. Ursula is in the top 1% because both parents have a graduate or professional degree, and Eleanor is in the top 6% because of her mother's MBA and the top 1% because her father has a JD.

If we use parental income, we get another answer. Whitney Page's mother earns about $25,000 a year, which places her in the working/

poverty class. The U.S. median individual income for a female high school graduate was $21,219 in 2007 (U.S. Census Bureau, 2007), and 20% of U.S. families made under $27,800 in 2008. Louise's parents make $50,000. Forty percent of U.S. families made under $49,325 in 2008 (U.S. Census Bureau, 2008b). Misty's parents are businesspeople and have a combined income of $140,000, which is average for one parent with a bachelor's degree and one parent with a master's degree. Eighty percent of U.S. families made less than $113,025 in 2008 (U.S. Census Bureau). Ursula's parents have a combined income of $200,000, which is about average for a physician and a professor in their state. This amount is the lower boundary of the upper 5% of U.S. family income (U.S. Census Bureau). Eleanor's parents don't work, so the source of their income is not the same as it is for the other parents.

If we ask college students they will say that Whitney Page is working class; Louise, Misty is middle class; Ursula is upper-middle class; and Eleanor is definitely upper class.

If we use Bourdieu's (1986) economic, cultural, and social capitals as a way to assign class on campus to each of these students, we get a way to illustrate the differences between these women as seen in Figure 4.

Whitney Page has low capital across the board. College access scholarships will address her economic need, but where will she find the cultural and social capital to succeed on campus? Remember, if class is seen as economic, then the solution to class inequities is economic. Louise has moderate economic capital in comparison to all U.S. families but low compared to students on campus. As with Whitney Page, Louise will need to develop her own cultural and social capital, and the financial aid office staff will help her with economic capital on campus. Misty has moderate cultural capital compared to the general undergraduate population, and she has social skills and a limited social circle.

## What will likely happen to these women?

Where will each of these students go to college, and will she be successful?

FIGURE 4
**Levels and Types of Capital**

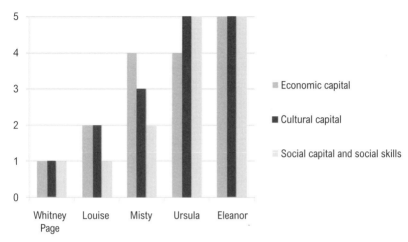

The statistical probable answer is that Whitney Page may go to a community college if she goes at all, and she is not likely to graduate. Louise will probably go to a community college or to a state college with open access and may graduate. Misty will go to TFSU and is likely to graduate. Ursula and Eleanor will go to highly selective colleges, probably Ivy League or Seven Sisters, and will probably graduate within four years. The bleak reality of Whitney Page's and Louise's probable failure to get a college degree is supported by the mass of data about students like them. You have your own interpretations, but you don't get your own data. Is it any wonder that highly selective Ivy League/Seven Sisters colleges have such high graduation rates with students like Ursula and Eleanor, or that community colleges and open-access colleges have such a low graduation rate with students like Whitney Page and Louise?

People seem to genuinely like Whitney Page and Louise and want them to succeed, but on campus students and faculty act as though Whitney Page and Louise are outsiders who need to learn the manners, norms, and rules that Misty, Ursula, and Eleanor learned at home. This is one way of saying that Whitney Page and Louise's social class of origin is negatively sanctioned, or that Whitney Page's and Louise are oppressed. Whitney Page and Louise don't really feel comfortable being on campus, even on an open-access university with many other first-generation students. The people on campus in the majority social class make Whitney Page and Louise uncomfortable. The consequence is that Whitney Page and Louise don't feel like they fit in; they feel like imposters. When they are on campus, Whitney Page and Louise are outside their class bubble as much as Misty is inside hers. Even if they find a refuge on campus with people like them, their experiences in the larger environment will still be stressful. The stress may be enough to convince each of them to return to the comfort of home and the familiarity of their class bubble.

Few people worry about the pressure on Ursula and Eleanor to excel socially and academically. Few people seem concerned with the stress and anxiety both women will experience as they work hard to meet their perceived family expectations. A common response is, "The Eleanors are rich, so they don't have problems." While people genuinely like Ursula and recognize her cultural capital, they aren't concerned about her in the same way they seem concerned about Louise.

People don't seem to like Misty and see her as spoiled. In most stories about Misty's future, people predict that she will join a sorority, find a husband, have an easy major, graduate, and move back to the suburbs. There is a sense of her moral inferiority in these assumptions about Misty. She doesn't work hard and doesn't appreciate things. Misty's problems are dismissed: "Isn't it tragic when inconvenient things happen to privileged people?" Louise, on the other hand, is seen as having to work hard, which gives her some moral superiority.

Ursula is not wealthy, but her experiences distance her from the students, faculty, and staff who typically have far less cultural capital and have traveled less than she has. Ursula uses her social skills to make friends with everyone, bridging the class gap. As a first-year student Ursula is already seen as a woman of accomplishment. She was given a leadership scholarship by her highly selective Seven Sisters' campus in recognition of her cultural capital that will make her one of tomorrow's leaders. The rich get richer.

Eleanor has celebrity status on campus, which makes her an object in many people's eyes rather than a first-year student or a young woman. For many students, faculty, and staff, Eleanor's social class status is the primary identity they see. People have ambivalent feelings about Eleanor. On campus they defer to Eleanor, privileging her for her economic, cultural, and social capital.

## Money, culture, and social class of origin

None of these women chose their parents or chose their circumstances. Resources to build cultural capital, travel, and visit exotic locales are not an issue for Misty, Ursula, and Eleanor because they can rely on family money. Yet Misty has not taken advantage of the same kinds of opportunities to travel and study abroad that Ursula embraced. Money is available for Whitney Page and Louise through many philanthropic organizations to help them take advantage of study abroad experiences even in high school, but the choice to work and help the family bank account is a strong incentive to stay at home rather than study in Spain. These five women are their parents' children. They learned their place in the world from their family, accumulating certain kinds of capital at home. For Whitney Page and Louise the knowledge and skills of their social class of origin are not needed on campus.

## Social class contrast and fit on campus

The view of class as something internal, some socially constructed identity, gives rise to an interesting analysis. When colleges are seen as having a social class culture, the idea of a person–environment fit becomes a tool to examine the student and the campus. For first-generation and lower social class students, college can be seen as a *middle classing*, or conversion, experience. The mismatch between students and the campus majority social class culture creates a tension that leads first-generation students and lower-class students to resist these differences, assimilate, or leave the campus (Pascarella, Pierson, Wolniak, &

Terenzini, 2004; Pascarella, Wolniak, Pierson, & Terenzini, 2003; Terenzini, Springer, Yaeger, Pascarella, & Nora, 1996). The class contrast for the first-generation student is an ever present challenge on campus, and finding ways to support minority class students on a majority class campus is hard.

For second-, third-, and fourth-generation students college may be seen as a confirmation experience. The majority class culture on campus resonates with these students' social class of origin. Dress, dialect, manners, methods of interaction, and organization on campus seem normal to the student from the majority class group. The college experiences for these students provide no class contrast and lead to an ongoing ignorance of class. Finding ways for majority class students to encounter class is hard, like trying to teach a fish about water.

The social class contrast between the lower-class student and the upper-class campus is akin to the experiences of ethnic minority students on predominantly majority campuses. Stephen Hess (2007) writes about the social contrast experiences of students at a highly selective private college. Kaufman (2003) examined social class reproduction and social class transformation in the context of a student's experiences at college, focusing on the noneconomic factors of interpersonal activities like language and dress. Berger (2000) used Bourdieu's theory as an analytical tool to examine student persistence and social class reproduction on campus, concluding that social class contrast is a significant issue for some students. Granfield (1991) examined this student-campus class match using Goffman's idea of stigma management. Kaufman examined how "working class individuals construct middle class identities" (p. 481) providing further insight about social class contrast.

The idea of contrast is campus specific. Obviously, the social class climate at Boston College is quite different from the social class climate at Indiana State University, and the experiences of first-generation students will be quite different on each of these campuses. No matter the location or the campus, social class contrast between students' current felt social class and the campus social class climate is a significant source of conflict.

## Experience

Take an hour during the day and look at the world through a social class lens. As you automatically assign gender and ethnicity to people you also assign social class. Be aware of what class you assign to each person, and make a conscious effort to pay attention to why you assign a person to a particular class. Was it dress, speech, stance, shoes, purse?

## Reflection questions

What part of talking about class makes you uncomfortable?
What part are you comfortable with?
What part of talking about class makes you angry?
Do you assign a different class to your instructors or your administrators than you do to other students?
Can you tell the social class of origin of other students in your classes?

## Discussion questions

Should there be a single simple definition of class or multiple definitions of class?
Which of the models of class presented in this chapter appeal to you the most?
Who should define social class and name the social classes?
How is class invisible and how is class visible?
What are some examples of upper-class behavior and what are some examples of lower-class behavior?
What are some other ways to talk about social class?
Do you live in a class bubble with most of your friends whose social class is similar to yours, or do you have lots of friends from different social classes?
Do you know people who are like each of the five women presented as examples?
In what ways are you like any of the five characters in this chapter?

Do you think people respond differently to class in women than they do to class in men?

Have you purchased anything, like a car or a phone or clothing, that you thought other people would see as a sign of your high or higher social class?

What are the markers for fashion, like certain labels or accessories or cars or phones, that reflect a lower-class character?

# CHAPTER 2

## *Your Experience and Social Class*

YOUR EXPERIENCE OF SOCIAL CLASS is yours and is relevant in your life. Your experience of class is not necessarily generalizable to the social class experiences of others, even to those in the same social class. Whitney Page, Louise, Misty, Ursula, and Eleanor have quite different experiences in the world, and their views on class reflect that. Not only are our experiences of class different, our definitions of class are different. In some ways social class is like photons. I am not a physicist, but I know of four different ways to describe a photon—wave, particle, Feynman's model, and string theory—and I suspect there are even more models of photons. While I enjoy photons on a daily basis, I cannot say there is a single clear definition for them. Where you start in your search for photons determines what you find. We were taught that in high school.

Social class is like the elephant explored by the seven blindfolded students who each touched a part. For some the experience was about the front of the elephant, for others it was about the rear of the elephant, and for still others the experience was about the sides of the elephant. For all the blindfolded students the experience was about the outside of the elephant. Where you start your search for the elephant determines what you find. This is the fourth sound bite, the fourth sticky idea in this book: Where you start in your search for class determines what you find.

## The Privilege Meme

The primacy of the personal point of view about class became very clear when the *Privilege Meme* hit the Internet. This was initially designed as a face-to-face experience to use on a U.S. campus called "What privilege do you have?" Created as a student and staff development exercise to increase participants' awareness of social class on campus, the experience was composed of a collection of statements that reflected what it was to have resources and consequently privilege. The statements were all based on research-based literature on class. The underlying concept of such a list of privileges was built on Peggy McIntosh's (1988) "White Privilege and Male Privilege: A Personal Account of Coming to See Correspondences Through Work in Women's Studies."

N. Jeanne Burns at http://quakerclass.blogspot.com/ transformed this classroom experience on privilege into an Internet-based experience listing each statement about privilege. People were invited to copy the list of privileges, highlight the privileges they had, add comments, and post them on their blogs and personal websites. This list was copied, forwarded to others, posted on blogs, and commented on widely. Most of the initial postings were on individual blogs, and most of the comments were positive, although some were quite negative. What was surprising was the emotional responses, positive and negative. People's negative comments typically noted that some particular privilege statement was not a valid marker of class in their experience; thus, the entire list was invalid.

## Where you start matters

If you come to understand class based on your personal experiences, your understanding of class will be limited until you learn more about the class experiences of others. If you come to understand class on a journey to understanding ethnicity, then you will have a view of class heavily influenced by ethnicity. While class and ethnicity are closely related, starting at ethnicity and moving to class will result in very different views of class than if you start at class and move toward ethnicity. Which is more important, class or ethnicity? This is the screwdriver question, and the answer depends on the context of the question. Asking if certain students will go to college, where they will go, and if they will graduate are different questions from asking about the daily oppression experienced by ethnic minorities.

If you come to understand class on a journey to understanding education and income, you will have a view of class heavily influenced by education and income. While class, education, and income are closely related, starting at education and income will result in an incomplete view of class. Does education determine class, or does class determine education?

## Starting with boundaries

If you come to understand class by searching for class boundaries, will you look at demographics or at personal experience? Stuber (2005) noted that upper-middle-class students in her study were more sensitive to the class barriers above them than below them. I would assert, based on her study and on subsequent conversations about class, that upward class sensitivity is far more prevalent than downward class sensitivity. Awareness of what separates us from the class above us, however perceived, is easy and is found in most stories about class. Awareness of what separates us from the class below us seems lacking. The implication here is that the hierarchy of class is important to us and the classes below us are not nearly as important as those above us. By analogy this could be extended to mean that the people in the classes below us are not nearly as important as the people in the class above us. If you come to understand class by looking above your current felt social class you will get someplace other than if you come to understand class by looking below your current felt social class. If you come to understand class on a journey searching for boundaries, you will miss the territory between the borders.

If you come to understand class on a journey to understanding individuals, then you will have a view of class heavily influenced by individual psychology. A great deal of this book deals with class as a personal and interpersonal phenomenon. Class as identity, using the same conceptual models that underlie ethnicity as identity, is a root of a personal view about class and leads to a developmental and transitional view of class identity.

If you come to understand class on a journey to understanding groups, you will have a view of class heavily influenced by sociology, economics, political science, and campus ecology.

If you come to understand class from a Marxist or neo-Marxist perspective, you will have a view of class heavily influenced by social and economic forces.

## Starting somewhere

Each of these views of class has an advantage and a disadvantage, and none tells the entire story of class. While this book emphasizes viewing class from an individual perspective, balancing an individual view of class and a group view of class helps to more completely understand class on campus because of the multiple perspectives used. The emphasis in this book is the individual experience of class, but that must be understood within the larger cultural, social, economic, and political reality of higher education in the United States. Some of the concepts of this book will work in other nations and other cultures with the appropriate adjustments.

Gender is grounded in a biological reality. Ethnicity is in some way related to people's geographical origin. Social class has no basis in the physical world. My preferred definition of class uses a personal lens: I see class as something personal in each of us. Social class is your and my collection of attitudes, values, and behaviors reflecting a self-identified social group and a personal identity. These attitudes, values, and behaviors are deeply affected by your and my perceptions of prestige. Social class is viewed here primarily as a personal social construct; social class is based solely on what individual people believe to be true. Peoples' collective beliefs become common knowledge, implicit norms, tacit assumptions, and their constructed reality.

Treating social class as personal has advantages and disadvantages. One advantage is that the tools of identity, individual development, and individual difference can be used to understand class. A second advantage is that individual responsibility for class and the consequent interpersonal oppression takes the forefront. Social forces are a collection of individual actions. When class is seen as personal, our individual actions become important. One disadvantage of viewing class as personal is that large-scale social and economic forces cannot be easily managed. Abstracting from the personal to social forces is important, and the usefulness of analyzing social forces is well established. A disadvantage of a social forces view of class is that it removes the personal. If social forces perpetuate class, the actions of the individuals behind these social forces recede into abstraction. Obviously, multiple views of class work best.

## Historical views of class

Class, or ranking people in a hierarchy, dates from a long time ago. Recorded history and archeological evidence tell us that societies are typically organized into hierarchical groups: rulers, theologians, laborers, scribes, slaves, farmers, tradespeople, and so on. Membership in these groups has historically been hereditary, and one's membership created one's identity. You were born into a group in the social hierarchy and there you stayed. Your *station in life*, the idea that you are born into a group and that is where you stay, has long been a mechanism to ensure social stability. In the words of Mel Brooks (1981) in the movie *History of the World: Part I*, "It's good to be the king." Getting to create the hierarchy of stations in life based on gender, ethnicity, birthright, hair color, or any criteria is a powerful method of social control. Being among the group that creates and maintains class structure is a powerful social position.

Changing classes was uncommon for most of human history. Hero tales of individuals rising in status through dream interpretation, strength, intelligence, artistic ability, or whatever are noteworthy because of their uncommonness. Stories of people remaining potters or scribes or laborers are not the stuff of legend. In the famous Horatio Alger (1869/2010) story of luck and pluck changing class always involved the intervention of someone from the upper classes—that is the luck part. Pluck was the hard work part. Alger's characters and historical heroes needed a patron from the upper classes. In the college context luck is admission to the highly selective prestige campus that has an excellent mentoring program.

*Plato and class.* In *The Republic* Plato (trans. 1945) divided the population into three races: gold (rulers and holders of wisdom), silver (auxiliaries), and bronze/brass and iron (artisans). Plato's concept is based on Hesiod's earlier conceptualization of an ideal civilization, and they both argue against mixing the metals. Contextualizing this in Greek society in which slavery was a fact of everyday life, the slaves become the laborers and are never counted among the classes. In contemporary discussions of class is it any wonder that the members of the underclass in the United States, the poverty class and working class, are rarely mentioned, and that the emphasis is on the middle class whatever that may be?

*Christianity and class.* Matthew 19:24 (Jerusalem Bible) in the New Testament is one of the classic Christian references to social class: "I tell you the truth, it is hard for a rich man to enter the kingdom of heaven. Again I tell you, it is easier for a camel to go through the eye of a needle than for a rich man to enter the kingdom of God." The theology and social context of this quote is worthy of study; nevertheless, it is clear that referring to the rich or the poor as a member of a class was and is well understood by the speaker and writer of the text and its audience and reader.

*China and class.* The dynastic Chinese civil service examinations were one way for commoners to achieve status, prestige, power, and wealth. A high score on the exam made it possible to receive a government position that provided opportunities for power and wealth. However, having the time and resources to study the required texts, as well as the training to read and write, assumed a certain level of wealth that was undoubtedly out of the reach of the common Chinese of that day.

*Hindu and class.* The Vedas, which are sacred Hindu texts, described the Hindu caste system in detail giving rise to thousands of years of a hereditary and divinely ordained social order in Hindu cultures. The highest caste, or class, were the priests and teachers (Brahmin), then the rulers and warriors (Kshatriya), followed by the merchants, craftsmen, and farmers (Vaishyas), and finally in the lowest caste the servants (Shudras). The Boston Brahmin, the scions of old New England who traced their ancestry to original settlers, took (or were given) their name from this hereditary and divinely ordained caste tradition of India. Extending the caste idea to include the lower class, I can only wonder which caste my New England ancestors were in because they were neither Pilgrims nor Puritans who were run out of Boston.

*Native Americans and class.* Cahokia Mounds Historic Site in Illinois, designated a World Heritage Site by the United Nations Education, Scientific, and Cultural Organization, is the remains of a city that may have reached a population of 40,000 in the 13th century, making it larger than any European city at the time. A key feature of this site is the Monks Mound, which represents a physical corollary to a class structure with physical separations of classes. Other early American sites contain similar features that segment the population and favor religious and government leaders.

The idea of class, or a hierarchical social ranking based on the possession of wisdom, wealth, knowledge, or birthright, is ubiquitous throughout history. Architectural sites and written documents demonstrate that class is a common part of human history. No doubt there are examples of classless societies, but those are the notable exceptions. If you begin learning about class as a group historical phenomenon then your view of class will have these group and historical overtones.

*Marx and Engels on class.* The two seminal works on the Marxist version of class are *The Communist Manifesto* (Marx & Engels, 1848/ 1954) and *Capital: A Critique of Political Economy* (Marx, 1906). These are often cited as key works on class and define the role of class in the industrial society. Even though they were written in a bygone historical, cultural, and economic context many scholars view the core concepts as currently relevant analytical economic and social tools. Seen in a historical context Marx sharpened the focus of politics on class, targeting especially labor and ownership of the means of production, and discussing the social consequences of the inequitable distribution of wealth and power. The ideas of Marx are explored in chapter 9. If you begin your exploration of class with the works of Marx, your view of class will have Marxist overtones.

Where you start matters.

## Class and anticlass

In classic views of ethnic identity development (Cross, 1995; Helms, 1995), after individuals encounter their identity status, like class or gender, they react to the majority identity by rejecting it. While exploring moral development and developing the defining issues test, James Rest (1979) discovered individuals at what he called stage 5A who had definite antiestablishment values but still participated in complex stage 5 moral reasoning. One of the ways students respond to an awareness of class is to reject trappings of class, or at least they stop participating in behaviors that are driven by their perceptions of class and act in a way that is the opposite of their current felt social class.

Dress, or costuming, to use the idea that class is a role, is a good example of how people can reject one role of class and adopt an alternative expression of that role. Zoot suits in the 1930s and 1940s are an ethnically based rejection of class and fashion, making the zoot suit a positive ethnic statement and a rejection of majority ethnic and class social norms. The zoot suit was antimajority class and antimajority ethnicity. There are classic black-and-white photos of Bennington College women in the 1940s and 1950s dressed in a manner that offended the townspeople because the women were not "well dressed." This is antifashion, which in that elite group of college women is really anticlass. The rejection of mainstream fashion by college students in the late 1960s and early 1970s is well documented in photographs of students from that era. Fashion and antifashion play out on campuses daily today. From one point of view wearing Carhartt is an authentic social class statement, and from another point of view it is an antifashion statement. For other students who didn't grow up in an agricultural community, to appropriate Carhartt is an antifashion statement that has very negative overtones.

## Key words and secret language

The language we use about class determines our view of class. Revealing the disguised dialogue about class requires knowing ways that class is disguised. Terms heard on campus like *first-generation students, access, legacy students, community colleges, selective colleges, need-based aid,* and *merit-based aid* are all class-based terms. Understanding the hidden meanings of language is a way to further understand class.

First-generation students is defined in two ways. First, a restrictive definition is students whose parents did not attend college at all; this group represents about half of all 18-year-olds and about one quarter of all students on four-year campuses. Second, a less restrictive definition is students whose parents did not complete college; this group represents about 72% of all 18-year-olds (U.S. Census Bureau, 2008a). Some authors wish to define first-generation students as a binary construct, making it something you are or are not, and emphasize the differences between the two groups. The difficulty with such a binary construct is that it doesn't reflect reality. Using a binary construct, a student with one parent who had one semester at community college is not grouped with first-generation students but is grouped with everyone else, from Misty to Eleanor. My preference is to use parental experience in the educational system as a matter of degree that falls somewhere between parents who have no experience in postsecondary education and parents who completed college.

Access describes the ability to enroll in and pay for college. Calls for increased access are heard from the political left, right, and center. After all, who is not in favor of more U.S. citizens' getting more education, having more income, and paying more taxes? Access reflects an attitude that everyone should want to improve his or her life through education. The unexamined assumption in the quest for an improved life is the belief that uneducated (poor) people have lives less worth living than do educated (rich) people, and the lives of the uneducated need improving. Those exhorting colleges to increase enrollment typically ignore the reality that nearly anyone who wants to go to a four-year college can get accepted somewhere in the state system. Admission may come with a heavy load of remedial courses that don't count toward graduation and with the possibility of college debt. Further, if one cannot get into a four-year college, community colleges are open to nearly everyone.

"Legacy students" has become code for the children of college graduates of a university—the opposite of first-generation students. Legacy students come from families with education, which means that family members know the norms of the campus life. Deconstructing this idea of legacy we find that legacy students come to campus knowing the secret handshakes, dress and behavior codes, and may well come to campus knowing select faculty and administrators. Is the percentage of legacy students at Harvard similar to the percentage of legacy students at less prestigious schools?

Community colleges, one of the success stories of U.S. education, is a code word for postsecondary institutions for the lower classes, for students not destined for management jobs and not destined for one of the traditional professions. The community college system does provide access and upward mobility and is a great national triumph. But it is important to recognize that only a small percentage of students who enroll at community colleges ever transfer to, much less graduate from, four-year colleges (Bradburn, Hurst, & Peng, 2001). Community colleges provide valuable commodity skills to enable students to become the skilled working class with low work autonomy and little supervisory authority in their work settings. A quick examination of the programs at community colleges reveals their core vocational curriculum. In some ways the community college system maintains the social class structure in the United States similar to the ways the four-year college system maintains social class structure.

Selective colleges is the code word for upper-middle and upper-class colleges. While community colleges are for the underclass, selective and highly selective colleges are for the higher class. Selective colleges get the highest rankings in the media. Somehow selectivity is synonymous with quality. Research indicates that selectivity brings a more well-educated and richer student to campus who graduates at a higher rate than students with lower-quality K–12 educations and less money (Sacks, 2007). Concurrently, *open-access university,* often used to describe the second- or third-tier state school, is a code word for lower-class campus.

Need-based and merit-based financial aid are class-loaded terms. Need-based financial aid refers to family income and is used to provide financial assistance to academically qualified students who don't have money. Merit-based financial aid is given to students with high grades, high test scores, and high academic class standing. These students are widely sought by selective colleges, and merit-based financial aid is one way to attract these students to a campus that reaps the consequent elevation in school rankings. Grades, test scores, and academic class standing are closely tied to social class. Merit-based aid is the code word for higher-class students and need-based aid is a code word for lower-class students. Many selective campuses are proud of their *need blind* aid and it is prominently advertised. This can be deconstructed as a declaration that lower-class students need not apply.

## Summary

The experience of class on campus is different for different groups. Men and women from the lower classes, however defined, are immediately faced with class contrast when they arrive on most campuses, and class contrast remains an everyday part of their college experience. The mismatch that lower class and first-generation students feel on campus is similar to ethnic minority students' experiences on predominantly ethnic majority campuses. The lack of social class contrast on campus for majority social class students makes their transition to campus life invisible and serves to confirm the upper-middle-class students' worldview.

Class is complicated. A simple view of class can lead to poor personal choices and poor public policy. If policy makers believe that class is about income, then their remedies for class-based problems will be money based. Similarly, if policy makers believe that class is about culture, their remedies for class-based problems will be educational and cultural. One of the hardest things to learn is something we think we already know. If you think you know all about social class, why would you want to learn more? If you think class is all about money, then learning that class is personal, cultural, and prestige will be a challenge. If you came to campus from a prestige background, seeing class will be difficult for you. To give you an idea about class, watch the original 1958 *Auntie Mame* (DeCosta, 1958) with Rosalind Russell and pay attention to how class is portrayed. If you want something more contemporary, watch *Crash* (Haggis, 2004) and pay attention to class messages.

## Experience

Write a personal classnography. What is your social class story?

1. When you were in elementary school, how did you identify your social class or your economic status? Were you rich, richer than some, poor, poorer than some, about average, or did you have no clue? This is a two-part question: One ·is to identify your social class of origin, and the other is to have you reflect on your awareness of class as money at that age.

2. How do you describe your current felt social class, and what are your reasons for identifying in that way? This is a way for you to identify how you think about, write about, sing about, or dance about class. What is class to you, and how do you use that to self-identify? This is a two-part question about awareness of class in your life now and about how you see class markers in your life.

3. Write about a time in your life, a critical incident perhaps, when you were very aware of social class.

4. Write about a time when you found yourself being jealous of someone else because of what he or she owned or his or her ability to participate in something that you couldn't because of money or class.

5. Write about a time when you had to change your vocabulary or mannerisms to communicate with someone from a different class.

6. Write about a time when someone told you that you are of a social class other than what you think you are.

## Reflection questions

What do you believe about social class?
Can people change their social class, either up or down?

## Discussion questions

Is everything classed, or are some things not associated with any social class?
What is the majority class group on your campus?
What are the social classes of origin for other people in your class?
What do you value in fashion, and how is that classed?
What are the visible markers or behaviors for members of the campus majority class?
What do other people in your classroom, especially those from a class different from yours, believe about social class?
How is class seen differently for European Americans, African Americans, Hispanic Americans, Asian Americans, and immigrants?
What class assumptions do people make about members of different ethnic groups?
What role does social class play in political affiliation? Are members of any political party or movement mostly from a particular class?

# CHAPTER 3

# Class Myths

ON THE WEBSITE www.steamiron.com/payday Cheryl Cline lists 25 things one hears when talking about class. Seven of these statements help illustrate points about class that are salient here, but all her points are worth serious thought and consideration.

## "Class doesn't exist in the USA."

This myth is the classic denial of class. No matter what model anyone uses for class, differences between Americans in income, education, occupational prestige, cultural capital, social capital, speech, dress, accessories, beverage preference, and even comedy preferences are dramatic. People lead their lives, go to school, go to work, shop, and play with people from their own class. Most of us read magazines and access media that reflect people like us. Hanging out with people like us is common. Ignorance of class can come from a lack of noticing our differences. Birds of a feather . . .

Without regular experiences across class boundaries, many of us find it easy to deny class. Denying class allows each of us to avoid dealing with class, class-based issues, and our own role in cocreating our classed society. The denial of class allows people to maintain the erroneous opinion that poor people are poor because they don't work hard, that we are all the same class, that some of us just work hard enough to have money. When Misty is immersed in a campus with people like her, class differences are hard for her to experience. This classic denial myth is typical of people in the majority class because the majority systems, norms, cultural attitudes, and fashion styles belong to the majority class. Anyone from a working-class or poverty-class background knows from personal experience that class is alive and well because he or she encounters it every day.

Cross (1995) wrote that encounter is the first stage on the road to awareness and change. Spending time with other people who believe this myth, who deny class, helps to reinforce the myth as a worldview. Challenging this myth and making class a foreground issue (Van Galen, 2000) is an important part of working for social justice and celebrating diversity.

## "We are all middle class anyway."

This myth recognizes the existence of class while simultaneously denying differences. Zweig (2000) and Van Galen (2000) define working class in terms of work autonomy, making the point that the vast majority of the working public has little work autonomy, which makes it working class. The media perpetuates this myth by referring to the "growing middle class" without being too specific about who belongs in that group. The upper class, the upper 20% in income, education, and occupation, magically disappears when it becomes labeled as part of the growing middle class. This upper 20% becomes the same as the middle class, but somehow slightly better. The renaming of the status of the upper 20% leads to all manner of complications, the least of which is understanding the role of this group in maintaining social class because of its economic, educational, and occupational status.

A great advantage to this magic of the top 20% disappearing by renaming the upper-middle class is that those in this 20% group are no longer in the so-called oppressor upper class; they are someone else, some other people, some ultra-rich elite, ultra-connected, ultra-secret people we read about in tabloids and conspiracy stories. An ultra-elite class does exist but there are very few people in this group. The reality is that 20% of us are in the top 20%, and because of that we should properly be called the upper class because we are in the upper group, regardless of the ultra-elite class.

By embracing the notion that everyone is the same, that everyone is middle class, we get to deny important differences. "Why can't we all get along?" "Doesn't all this talk about diversity lead to divisiveness?" This class-unifying myth creates a fictional homogeneous giant middle class that can become a political, social, or religious force.

In Garrison Keillor's fictional Lake Wobegon all the children are above average. This is true if you choose the right comparison group. Choosing the right comparison group, the elite rich, makes me upper-middle class. Comparing upward in class is classic. Choosing the right comparison group, the poorest 80% in family income, makes the top 20% well above average. It is easy to ignore the richest 19% of U.S. families when you pay attention to the 1% ultra-rich elite, ultra-famous media personalities.

## "The working class is disappearing."

This statement recognizes class, recognizes the differences between classes, and reflects an out-of-date worldview when work and physical labor were the same in the United States. Traditional working-class jobs have disappeared in the United States as labor-intensive manufacturing has relocated to areas of the world where wages are low. The laboring class in the United States is disappearing because of the global labor economy. The work of the working class has moved from labor jobs to service jobs. These new service-class jobs have traditional working-class characteristics: low wages, minimal work autonomy, and little or no supervision over others. Members of the modern working class now dress in more prestigious clothing and work in cubicles, yet they remain an underclass.

## "Once you get a degree you are no longer working class."

A Madame Alexander doll dressed in a graduation cap and gown is still a Madame Alexander doll. This myth recognizes the ubiquitous nature of class while believing that class mobility is as simple as graduation. A Madame Alexander doll's change in clothing, and the implied change in its status, does not change its identity as Madame Alexander. Dress the doll as a nuclear physicist or as a sanitation engineer and it is still a Madame Alexander doll with a change of clothes. The doll's identity does not change with its accomplishments as symbolized in its change of costume and role.

This myth casts class as something external to the individual. This myth does not recognize the very real changes that class shift engenders in identity and relationships. When class change is seen as the result of getting a diploma, something external that may or may not reflect an internal change, the idea of someone having an internal and individual social class as part of identity and culture is ignored.

## "Education is the key to upward mobility."

The best propaganda campaign is misinformation. All great lies start with a truth. The best propaganda is 90% accurate. The best misinformation appears to be true and is something people want to believe. Education is certainly one key to upward mobility, but the reality is more complicated, and the complication is what makes this a myth. The report "A Test of Leadership: Changing the Future of U.S. Higher Education" (U.S. Department of Education, 2006) repeats the idea that education is the key to upward mobility. One of the cornerstones of the report is promoting access to postsecondary education because rising college costs and shrinking financial aid are an impediment to increased access. The report ignores the fact that college costs and enrollments continue to rise.

Education is the key to upward mobility for many, but it's just not that simple. Lower-prestige occupations like teaching and nursing are filled with people who are first-generation students, whose parents never attended college or attained a degree. While it is true that first-generation students become college professors and physicians, the typical reality is that education helps people up the ladder of occupational prestige, educational attainment, and income one rung at a time.

This myth also has the hidden assumption that education leads to success, which is a debatable point. Education is not working for many people. It is not their key to upward mobility. Americans have a high school graduation rate between 75% and 85% depending on which study you read. Census data on educational attainment in the United States in 2008, as shown in Figure 5 and Figure 6, are revealing.

People without a high school diploma don't go to college (with a very small number of exceptions). The reality is that public high

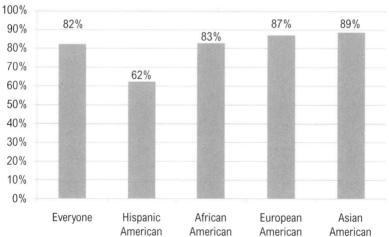

### FIGURE 5
### High School Graduation Attainment of Adults Over 25 by Ethnicity in 2008

Note. Adapted from *Educational Attainment in the United States: 2009. Detailed Tables, Table 1 of the Population of 18 Years and Over, by Age, Sex, Race, and Hispanic Origin*, by U.S. Census Bureau, 2009.

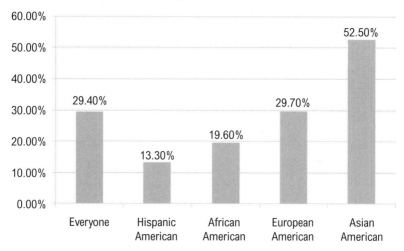

**FIGURE 6**
**College Degree Attainment Rates of Adults**
**Over 25 by Ethnicity in 2008**

*Note.* Adapted from *Educational Attainment in the United States: 2009 Detailed Tables, Table 1 of the Population 18 Years and Over by Age, Sex, Race, and Hispanic Origin,* by U.S. Census Bureau, 2009.

schools are failing to educate nearly one in four students to reach the level of high school graduation. Most of the students who do not graduate are poor. There is a strong relationship between school district income and graduation rates (Cataldi, Laird, KewalRamani, & Chapman, 2009). One interpretation is that public schools are in the business of preventing upward mobility of poor students. The truth is much more complicated.

## "College is open to anyone who wants to work hard."

Access to college and the transition from high school to college are rarely tied to issues of class. While about 55% of U.S. adults over 25 have some college experience, only about 25% of the four-year college population has parents with no college experience. Children of college graduates are far more likely to do well in high schools, go to college, and graduate than children from families with no parental college experience (NCES, 2005).

Assuming that intelligence is distributed randomly in a population, which is most likely true, leads to an interesting question. If children from wealthy families are no more intelligent than children from poor families, why is it that children from poor families generally do worse in school than children from wealthy families? While it is tempting to assume that children from wealthier families are smarter, this is just not the case. "Some people are born on third base and go through life thinking they hit a triple" (this wonderful quote is attributed to football coach Barry Switzer). Should we attribute the lack of success of children from poor families to individual effort—that children from poor families don't work as hard, that these children have bad parents and home environments that don't support learning—or should we be asking about the interaction between the children from poor families and their teachers?

## "You can't separate class from ethnicity."

In discussions about class this myth is bound to appear. This is not one of Cline's list of 25 myths, but comes from my experiences in talking about class. Like most myths, it is true and it is false. It would seem on the surface that the discussion should be about the relative effects and interactions between class and ethnicity. The direction of the discussion should depend on the context of the question. Unfortunately, this myth is often used to minimize the importance of class and to maximize the importance of ethnicity. Many times when this myth appears in a conversation it is assumed that since class and ethnicity are inseparable the primary discussion should focus on ethnicity. Much like the choice of screwdrivers, which one we choose should depend on how we plan to use the analytical lens.

Believers in this myth often equate class and ethnicity, generalizing inappropriately about ethnic groups and their class. Not everyone from the same ethnic group comes from the same class. Not all members of each class come from the same ethnic group. This denial of diversity within ethnic groups is an unexamined assumption. Stereotyping all members of one ethnic group as poor, as is often the case with generalizations about African Americans, has dangerous consequences. Income is not distributed equally across ethnic groups. By percentage of their population there are more lower-income African Americans and Hispanic Americans than European Americans. By absolute numbers there are more poor European Americans than African Americans or Hispanic Americans. Asian Americans have the highest standardized test scores and the highest incomes. There are high- and low-income people in every ethnic group.

Being a poor African American is a different experience than being a poor Asian American, a poor Hispanic American, or a poor European American. The reality of differences within groups should lead to a discussion of the interaction of class and ethnicity rather than perpetuating the myth that class and ethnicity are so similar as to be inseparable.

## "All White people are the same."

Looking at the myths of Whiteness with the lens of prestige helps illuminate the intermixing of class and ethnicity. Whiteness is a modern fabrication that can be deconstructed using prestige as a lens. Not all origins of Whiteness are equal. The origins of Whiteness are clearly European; however, different European origins have different prestige values.

A simple experiment will clarify this. The current list of European nations is shown in Table 1. You can rank the nations according to what you think is their generally perceived order of prestige, but make sure not to give in to national pride. Or you can rank the nations by prestige as you think others would rank them. You can assign each nation to one of five categories from high prestige (1) to low prestige

### TABLE 1
### European Nations 2011

| | | |
|---|---|---|
| Albania | Georgia | Netherlands |
| Andorra | Germany | Norway |
| Armenia | Greece | Poland |
| Austria | Hungary | Portugal |
| Azerbaijan | Ireland | Romania |
| Belarus | Italy | Russia |
| Belgium | Kazakhstan | San Marino |
| Bosnia and Herzegovina | Latvia | Serbia |
| Bulgaria | Liechtenstein | Slovakia |
| Croatia | Lithuania | Slovenia |
| Cyprus | Luxembourg | Spain |
| Czech Republic | Macedonia | Sweden |
| Denmark | Malta | Switzerland |
| Estonia | Moldavia | Turkey |
| Finland | Monoco | Ukraine |
| France | Montenegro | United Kingdom |
| | | Vatican City |

(5). Or you can just read the list and mentally pick out the high-prestige nations and the low-prestige nations. Not all nations have equal prestige.

While rankings will vary, the results will depend on familiarity, perception, and stereotypes, which drive prestige notions about Whiteness. Ethnicity and class are intertwined at the level of prestige, stereotype, and familiarity. Name three cities in England, and then name three cities in the Ukraine, Kazakhstan, and Hungary. Does the prestige media cover fashion shows in Ljubljana, or Trieste, or Pécs?

What happened to last names at Ellis Island? Why did my mother-in-law change her name from Buchdrucker to Burke? Why do actors have stage names more like mine than like Ramón Gerardo Antonio Estévez and Alphonso D'Abruzzo? While the give-and-take of ethnicity and names (Levitt & Dubner, 2006) is certainly dynamic, prestige and bigotry (the inverse of prestige) about names has a long history in the United States. Whiteness as an ethnicity is complex. Being a descendant of people from northern and western Europe gives you more nation-of-origin prestige within Whiteness than if you came from other areas. Does Eurocentric mean all of Europe, or does Eurocentric mean England, France, and Germany?

The relationship between class and ethnicity is complex. While the discussion of this relationship often focuses on the issues of African Americans as a group and social class, focusing the discussion on European Americans as a group and social class is very illuminating.

## "People talk about class because they don't want to confront ethnicity and gender."

This myth comes from my experiences in talking about class. It is heard in conversations with people engaged in diversity work and arises from the ways people have learned diversity, from the models of diversity that people use, and from our own ego investment in our socially constructed identities. Deconstructing this myth is simple; the underlying idea of this myth is that the only diversities that matter are ethnicity and gender. This myth has the implication that discussions about class are irrelevant and serve only to detract from the important issues of ethnicity and gender. The context of the question determines the relative importance of gender, ethnicity, and class.

A second source of this myth is personal identity. Articulating our own identities and understanding and accepting others' identities is a big part of diversity education. A brief reflection demonstrates that the identities explored by the diversity industry are ethnicity and gender. Anyone who has been in any kind of diversity learning experience will have been sensitized in a positive way, I hope, to gender and ethnicity. This is a good thing. This is an important thing. This is not the only thing. Most people have a strong gender identity and a strong ethnic identity and a strong class identity, and strong other identities like religion, family relationships, or work role identity. The diversity education industry has framed diversity in certain ways, and adding new forms of diversity creates resistance. Making ethnicity and gender and class visible can be done in positive ways, leading to acceptance and understanding, or in negative ways, leading to alienation, discrimination, and hate.

## "Everyone knows about class."

This is perhaps the most pernicious myth of all. Like any effective misinformation, it is almost true and wholly believable. One of the hardest things to learn is something we think we already know. We learned about money and class in school. A moment's application of critical thinking skills reveals that schools are complex class-based organizations that are de facto and de jure designed to perpetuate class. Any school-based teaching about the nature of class should be immediately suspect. Even this book.

If I think I know something, if I believe I know something, then I don't need to learn more. Being satisfied in my ignorance by thinking and believing that I know something about class is an ineffective way to be present in a dynamic world. Knowing more about class, as with many important topics, is a more effective way to be in the world.

## "The world is a meritocracy."

This is true, but in an odd way. The reality is that the world of work, the world of college access, the world of college success is a meritocracy, but the trick is to understand what counts as merit. While it appears that academic achievement, standardized test scores, and extracurricular activities are the measures of merit (note that all of these are related to parental income), other subtle measures of merit count. At highly selective colleges the measures of merit include social class factors. Leadership experiences, out-of-school volunteer experiences, school-related activities, summer workshops, years spent abroad are all factors that enhance an application to a highly selective college. Participating in these experiences that build cultural capital takes money and time. If the poor need to work after school and in the summer, they are just out of luck. The rich get richer through these experiences. The world is a meritocracy, and evidence of class counts as merit.

## Myth and reality

The truth about class is much more complex than the myths about class. It is easier to blame poor people for their lot in life, for their lack of education, money, resources, and for their poor manners than it is to understand the underlying systems of class that perpetuate this situation. It is much easier to understand the underlying systems of class than to accept personal responsibility for the cocreation and perpetuation of class systems. Falk (2001) uses the idea of achieved stigma in which people are blamed for their lot in life as a convenient and common way to look at class and individuals. His alternative idea of existential stigma, in which a person's condition is seen as the result of circumstances beyond control, is another common way to look at class and individuals. This leads to blaming rich people for keeping the poor in their place. Myths about class should be examined in light of achieved stigma and existential stigma.

We should all reflect on our roles and actions in perpetuating class, in facilitating class movement, and in facilitating the acceptance of multiple class norms on campus.

## Experience

Watch a popular movie like *Auntie Mame* (DeCosta, 1958), *My Man Godfrey* (La Cava, 1936), *My Fair Lady* (Cukor, 1964), *The Devil Wears Prada* (Frankel, 2006), *Mr. Deeds* (Brill, 2002), or *Crash* (Haggis, 2004) through a class lens, paying particular attention to how class is represented and to the interaction between characters from different social classes.

## Reflection question

What was your emotional reaction as you read each of the class myths?

## Discussion questions

Do you think the author was fair in selecting these class myths?

Which of the class myths listed in this chapter do you believe are not myths but are true?

What other things do you think people believe about class that are not true?

How are the class myths listed in this chapter relevant in your current life?

Which of these class myths did you believe before reading this chapter?

Provide examples for at least one of these class myths from your experience on campus.

Who are really the ruling class? Are they the people who directly influence our lives like bankers, physicians, teachers, professors, and lawyers, or are they people with serious wealth who are invisible and have quiet influence in our lives?

Some people argue that social class is disappearing as an important diversity issue. Do you agree or disagree, and why?

# CHAPTER 4

# The Social Class Identity

WHERE YOU START MATTERS. Beginning with Whitney Page, a woman from the poverty class (family of five with an income below $25,790 in 2009) who will be a first-generation student, leads to one view of social class identity. Similarly, beginning with Louise or Misty or Ursula or Eleanor leads to other views of social class identity. Beginning with the experiences of a first-generation African American man from the poverty class leads to yet another view of social class identity. Beginning with the experiences of a sixth-generation Hispanic woman leads to another view of social class. Where you start matters.

All these starting points are important. Identity and identity development have been an important part of higher education and student development theory, research, and practice for a long time. Marcia (1966, 1967, 1994), Erikson (1968), Chickering (1972), Josselson (1987), and Chickering and Reisser (1983) are commonly cited in adult development literature. Evans, Forney, Guido, Patton, and Renn (2010) almost entirely exclude class as an identity. McEwen's chapter (2003) references models of racial, sexual, and gender identity development and briefly covers ability/disability, social class, religion, and geographic origin identity. Torres, Howard-Hamilton, and Cooper (2002) review models of identity development from multiple perspectives, with only a few references to social class. A ProQuest search of social science journals from 1999 to 2009 reveals that the word *gender* appears in 50,906 articles, *ethnicity* appears in 22,455 articles, *social class* appears in 8,364 articles, *SES* (socioeconomic status) appears in 22,314 articles, and *socioeconomic status* appears in 9,674 articles. Adding *identity* as a search term keeps the ranking the same. The conclusion is that gender identity and ethnic identity are far more widely studied than social class identity in spite of research on first-generation students (Pascarella et al., 2003; Pascarella et al., 2004; Terenzini et al., 1996) that identified social class–related issues as an important factor in college student success and retention.

## Social class identity: Development

Each of our identities, from social class to gender to ethnic to spiritual and to all the other identities, involves a constant developmental process. We begin with unawareness, moving to awareness and then moving toward integration. Simply put, you discover who you are, a process of identification, and who you are not, a process of differentiation. You choose a set of behaviors, attitudes, thoughts, and feelings about who you are and who you are not. You learn how to perform your gender role, your ethnic role, your class role, and all your other life roles. The more experiences you accumulate and the more you reflect on these experiences the more deeply you integrate your gender and ethnic and social class and all your other identities with each other and within your life.

The discovery of who you are and who you are not forms the basis for your identities. You notice how those around you who are like you act, eat, talk, dance, and behave in the world, and how you act, eat, talk, dance, and behave like that. You notice how those around you who are unlike you act, eat, talk, dance, and behave, and how you don't act like that. By imitating appropriate others you learn how to be a girl and eventually a woman and how not to be a boy or a man. You learn how to be a boy and eventually a man and how not to be a girl or a woman. You learn how to be Catholic and not any other religion, you learn how to be Jewish and not any other religion, or you learn how to be Methodist and not any other religion. You learn how to be White and not anything else, or how to be European American and not anything else, or Black and not anything else, or African American and not anything else, or Hispanic and not anything else, or Korean American and not anything else. You learn how to perform your social class and how not to perform other social classes. Kaufman (2003), writing about the sociology of social class transformation, uses the term *associational embracement* to reflect this identification process and *associational distancing* to describe this process of differentiation.

Family members, friends, and kids in school let you know if you are acting wrong by calling you names like sissy, tomboy, or some other epithet. Your learned behaviors are reinforced by those around you and become deeply internalized. Social class identification is reinforced subtly and overtly in marketing, educational aspirations, beer preference, brand preference, and the media. Romance stories about love across political and social classes are a Hollywood staple. *Pretty Woman* (Marshall, 1990) is one good example of class contrast transition in film. *Romeo + Juliet* (Luhrmann, 1996) is about love across political and business barriers. What would the story be like if Romeo was wealthy and Juliet poor? What would the story be like if Juliet was wealthy and Romeo was poor?

## Social class identity: Maturity

The process of experience, reflection, and integration is central to developing a more mature identity. In an ideal world, you continually have new experiences, reflect on them, and mature. If you live in a gender bubble, an ethnic bubble, or a class bubble, your experiences will not challenge you, and you will not reflect on them, and you will not mature. The college years provide a source of experiences that can lead to reflection and awareness and can result in integration. Experiences are all around us, but awareness requires that you pay attention. Whitney Page and Louise and Ursula and Eleanor are confronted every day with social class contrast on campus. Misty and majority class students can have the same in-class experience as Whitney Page or Louise, but for Misty the in-class experiences, discussion, expectations, and references to Paris landmarks are normal. Misty's attention isn't drawn to the classed nature of these experiences because there is no class contrast for her. If Misty does not pay attention, she does not get an awareness of class.

My gender identity has changed as I have aged, as I have accumulated new experiences as I have reflected on my life and as I have integrated this new learning into my everyday life. My current identity as a man is quite different from when I was 20, 30, or 40. Living in other cultures has provided me with the contrast that highlights gender, ethnicity, and class. Seeing the performance of masculinity in other cultures has challenged my ideas of masculinity. My first reaction to gender performance in Thailand was negative because I interpreted Thai men's behavior as feminine and unmanly by my standards because I made sense of their behavior in my historical and cultural context. On reflection I added a few lines from their masculinity script to my masculinity script. I have changed how I perform gender, I have changed my masculine gender identity, and I have not changed my gender.

For Misty and majority social class students there is no easily observed social class contrast. Social class experiences will not be in the foreground. Misty and all students at TFSU will experience obvious gender contrast, they will experience obvious ethnic contrast, and they will experience obvious religious contrast. Misty and majority class students will not have obvious experiences of social class contrast on campus.

When you look closely, identity is more complicated than this, but these are the basics. Some people are caught in the margins between identity categories, or they have dual religious or ethnic identities or even dual class identities. I wonder how Rae Dawn Chong thinks of her ethnicity. Or does she think of her ethnicities?

## Social class identity: Transition

My social class of origin, my current felt social class, and my attributed social class are much the same as each other and much the same as they have always been. I have a more mature social class identity than I had as a youth, but I have always been the same social class.

Social class identity development and social class identity transition are different. Development is a more mature identity, a more integrated identity, a more aware identity, an identity integrated with behaviors. Transition is a movement between social classes. For Whitney Page and Louise college will be a significant experience that leads to social class identity transition. For Ursula and Eleanor college will be a significant experience that leads to a more mature social class identity.

Whitney Page has a poverty/working-class social class of origin identity. If she completes college and becomes a high school teacher, she will have undergone a social class transition in economic, cultural, and social capital and occupational prestige. Her current felt social class may still be in poverty/working class while her attributed social class will be middle- or upper-middle class. No longer will her social class of origin match her current felt social class and her attributed social class. Whitney Page is on her way to becoming what she was not, and this can lead to her internalizing class conflict as she adds a social class identity.

## Our three social class identities

We all have a social class of origin. This identity is much like our gender of origin identity and our ethnicity of origin identity, and we have it all our lives.

We all have a current felt social class, what we think of ourselves. This may be the same as our social class of origin or it may be different. Social class self-concept, social class self-image, and developmental mature or immature models of social class identity are all names for the same underlying idea, much like different models of a photon are all models of the same underlying phenomenon. Our social class history may be mobile or static, but we feel a social class identity today. Consider Whitney Page's Aunt Wanda, who works as the supervisor of a cleaning crew in a downtown upscale hotel. She has supervisory authority over other women at work, she has prestige in her church group, and she has prestige in her social group. Her current felt social class in all these settings will be quite high. Place Aunt Wanda in a management-run meeting at work where she represents the cleaning crews, and her current felt social class will reflect that social context. All the children of Lake Wobegon are above average, given the right comparison group.

We all have an attributed social class that is the other side of current felt social class because it is what others feel about your social class. When two people meet for the first time, the dance of demographics passes a myriad of cues between them. In short order we identify each other's gender, ethnicity, and social class. The physical, behavioral, and interpersonal cues for social class identification, the foundation for attributed social class, are part of the subtle and not so subtle background of a conversation. Granfield (1991) identified speech and dress as important social class markers that students adjusted to fit in with the majority campus social class culture.

What you wear and how you wear it sends social class messages. Sherlock Holmes (Doyle, 1887) in *A Study in Scarlet* notes,

> By a man's finger-nails, by his coat-sleeve, by his boots, by his trouser-knees, by the callosities of his forefinger and thumb, by his expression, by his shirt-cuffs—by each of these things a man's calling is plainly revealed. That all united should fail to enlighten the competent inquirer in any case is almost inconceivable. (p. 20)

Class markers have been systematized by Holmes for Watson's edification, much like class markers are systematized by today's advertising. An older but equally good scene comes from Mark Twain (1875/1981):

> The summer evenings were long. It was not dark, yet. Presently Tom checked his whistle. A stranger was before him—a boy a shade larger than himself. A new-comer of any age or either sex was an impressive curiosity in the poor little shabby village of St. Petersburg. This boy was well dressed, too—well dressed on a week-day. This was simply astounding. His cap was a dainty thing, his close-buttoned blue cloth roundabout was new and natty, and so were his pantaloons. He had shoes on—and it was only Friday. He even wore a necktie, a bright bit

of ribbon. He had a citified air about him that ate into Tom's vitals. The more Tom stared at the splendid marvel, the higher he turned up his nose at his finery and the shabbier and shabbier his own outfit seemed to him to grow. Neither boy spoke. If one moved, the other moved—but only sidewise, in a circle; they kept face to face and eye to eye all the time. (p. 7)

Twain marks all the features of observable attributed social class and the resultant interaction and conflict, which ends with the mystery boy losing a brawl. As introductory material for *Tom Sawyer* this firmly establishes his social class of origin, his attributed social class, and his attitude toward those in an attributed social class above him.

In a later chapter, Twain (1875/1981) introduces Huckleberry Finn:

Shortly Tom came upon the juvenile pariah of the village, Huckleberry Finn, son of the town drunkard. Huckleberry was cordially hated and dreaded by all the mothers of the town, because he was idle and lawless and vulgar and bad—and because all their children admired him so, and delighted in his forbidden society, and wished they dared to be like him. Tom was like the rest of the respectable boys, in that he envied Huckleberry his gaudy outcast condition, and was under strict orders not to play with him. So he played with him every time he got a chance. Huckleberry was always dressed in the cast-off clothes of full-grown men, and they were in perennial bloom and fluttering with rags. His hat was a vast ruin with a wide crescent lopped out of its brim; his coat, when he wore one, hung nearly to his heels and had the rearward buttons far down the back; but one suspender supported his trousers; the seat of the trousers bagged low and contained nothing, the fringed legs dragged in the dirt when not rolled up. (p. 42)

Again, Twain used attributes of social class, and attitudes of cross-class contact, to introduce the second major character in the book. Twain also used the device of Tom's friendship with Huck and the other boy's general attitude toward him to anchor the reader in a particular view of interclass relations. Similarly the introduction of Becky Thatcher is filled with class-based imagery and with cross-class relationship issues. Tom Sawyer puts on his best behavior when he courts Becky and meets Becky's father, Judge Thatcher.

A primary social class cue comes from speech patterns. Class is intimately related to the varieties of English. Accent, timing, vocabulary, grammar, word choice, and sentence construction are all class cues in American English. While the class cues are different in American English, British English, Indian English, and Nigerian English, class cues remain a central part of our language. Tom and Ray Magliozzi on the National Public Radio program *Car Talk* have classic regional accents that are not at all prestigious, and they have degrees from Massachusetts Institute of Technology that are very prestigious. Listening to their language, cadence, timing, vocabulary, and word choice leads the listener to an assumption about their social class, and therefore about their intellect. Part of the joy of the show is the mismatch between their variety of English and their massive knowledge of all things automotive.

Another behavioral cue comes from nonverbals. How you stand, how you sit, how you move, what you do with your hands, and how you shake hands are all culturally learned cues from our social class of origin. Imagine how an actor would physically play a role as a working-class character different from the way that actor would play the role as an upper-class character. Goffman (1959) explores the presentation of self in everyday life writing about the intentional and unintentional cues and roles. Attributed social class can be seen, among other ways, as assigning people to social roles as well as social categories. The actors in each social class have a specific script, different behaviors, different clothing, and different accents.

## Social class contrast

Social class awareness comes from encountering a social class contrast. Awareness should stimulate some internal dissonance that moves toward increased integration of a social class identity and worldview. The lack of social class contrast drives social class identity stability. Whitney Page and Louise on an Ivy League/Seven Sisters campus will experience high social class contrast, which may drive them to change behaviors, fashion, manners, and their variety of English to fit in, while

Misty at TFSU campus will experience little social class contrast, which may reinforce her social class identity because of its normality on the campus. Misty will probably find social class resonance with people like her on campus, with campus organizations, structures, and experiences familiar to her that enable her to maintain her class bubble. This bubble will serve to prevent experiences that lead to social class awareness.

## Social class transition

The social class challenge for Misty on campus is achieving awareness. The challenge for Ursula and Eleanor is not getting distracted with others' perceptions of them. The challenge for Whitney Page and Louise is how to respond to social class contrast and pressure to conform. Many students simply leave campus because the social class pressure is too great. Learning the cultural competencies required on campus can be overwhelming. Other students manage this conflict by a social class transition to their achieved or attributed social class. These ideas of current felt social class and attributed social class provide two ways to look at social class transitions, since each of these identities can change. Social class transition can be seen as attaining cultural competence in a new social class. The danger of social class transition is a long-term sense of not fitting in until new cultural competencies have been learned and internalized.

For students like Whitney Page and Louise, were they to attend an Ivy League/Seven Sisters college, social class contrast encounter, similar to that described by Cross (1978, 1991, 1995), occurs twice. The first encounter occurs during the first few weeks of school when the Whitney Pages and Louises perceive the contrast between their social class of origin and the campus majority social class. If Whitney Page or Louise has worked hard to fit in on the prestige campus and has internalized behaviors, attitudes, speech patterns, or other prestige social class markers this is a transformation of their current felt social class. A second encounter occurs when Whitney Page or Louise returns home to her social class of origin environment and experiences social class contrast with hometown friends and family. One classic experience is hearing, "Just because you can use all those big words doesn't make you better than me."

A strong social press to conform felt by social class minority students like Whitney Page and Louise creates an encounter experience similar to Cross's (1978, 1991, 1995) notion. If the campus pressure for normative majority social class appropriate behavior is strong, the student-campus encounter may be overwhelming and the student may leave campus. Whitney Page and Louise may feel too much stress as the result of the subtle negative sanctions for their language, their dress, and all their classed behaviors. If Whitney Page and Louise have a strong sense of self they may resist the campus pressure. Issues of self-efficacy and social support are obviously involved in how students respond to social class contrast, as well as the strength of their social class of origin identity.

## Managing multiple social class identities

*Alternation.* Alternation and integration are two common strategies Whitney Page or Louise can employ in social class transition. Creating two different current felt social class identities and using them in different contexts is alternation. This is a bicultural identity in which Whitney Page or Louise crosses social class borders and is culturally competent in both social classes. Initially this may seem like multiple personality disorder, but this is one way to have two roles with two scripts, one script for each social class setting. Alternation is the process best described as "yes, and . . ." Like bilingualism, the individual has competency in both social classes and appropriately follows the norms, values, attitudes, and behavioral patterns in context. LaFromboise, Coleman, and Gerton (1993) suggest that models of bicultural alternation reflect a healthy way to be bicultural. On the positive side alternating identities give the individual access to a wider social, intellectual, and paradigmatic base of multiple classed ways of being in the world. On the negative side having multiple identities in a culture that values single identities can cause problems in relationships with other people. If after graduation Whitney Page and Louise employ alternation as a lifestyle choice, their attitudes toward people in the classes they inhabit will be open and accepting.

*Integration.* A second strategy to resolve differences between social class of origin and attributed social class is integration. Integration maintains a single social class identity based on merging internalized norms of the social class of origin and the current achieved or attributed social class. This is the process of avoiding all stigmatized behaviors, language, food, and other social class marked items in either the social class of origin or current social class. Integration may be a strategy employed as transitional toward assimilation or may be a lifelong social class identity. In either case, social class identity is carefully constructed, and the individual is keenly aware of social class–based environmental cues, behaviors, attitudes, and so on. LaFromboise et al. (1993) listed seven cultural competencies when exploring the development of ethnicity and noted that integration assumes cultural competence in at least two social classes.

*Assimilation.* A third strategy is rejecting social class of origin and embracing attained and attributed social class. Rejecting attitudes, norms, values, and other features of an identity is not healthy and can lead to any number of psychological symptoms and relationship problems. Assimilation reduces the contrast and tension of everyday social experiences. Malcolm X (1965) used the idea of assimilation in describing the strategies employed by African Americans in an attempt to live in a majority culture. Woody Allen (1983) portrayed a character in *Zelig* who would change his physical appearance, his size, and even his ethnicity to blend in with his surroundings. Zelig is the ultimate in assimilation.

Assimilation is the process in which an individual takes on the manners, dress, attitudes, tastes, speech patterns, and such of the social class he or she has made the transition to. On campus this is most often a lower social class student assimilating to a higher social class environment. Granfield (1991) identified a set of strategies employed by lower social class students at a prestigious law school in which students came to dress and speak like their more prestigious peers after their second year. Further, the law students changed their career aspirations from social justice law to practicing in prestigious firms. This is a pattern of rejecting social class of origin identity. Ganfield used Goffman's (1959) concept of stigma to explain how some lower social class students viewed their social class of origin.

The implications for personal growth and development are centered on the rejection of the individual student's past. In assimilation students, parents, and friends become less central to the values in the students' lives, and attitudes toward childhood friends and even relatives are characterized by rejection.

*Accommodation.* A fourth strategy for negotiating social class of origin with current attributed social class is acceptance of social class of origin and a rejection of current achieved or attributed social class. Accommodation also reflects Malcolm X's (1965) terminology and is the strategy an individual takes to live in a new social class environment but retains social class of origin behaviors, speech patterns, manners, and seeks accommodation from the majority culture. There is an expectation that other people and the social systems will accommodate a diverse social class set of norms, behaviors, and values within that majority class culture. In Granfield's (1991) study this strategy was initially used by some of the lower-class students at the prestigious law school who continued to dress, speak, and act as they did at home. Most first-generation students report being proud of their social class of origin.

The most likely accommodations on campus are events and support services focused on first-generation minority students much like women's centers, African American centers, Hispanic American centers, and a full array of services targeted at traditional minority students on campus. It is unlikely that faculty members will accommodate authentic speech and writing norms of those from the underclass.

## Support for social class transition

The challenge of social class contrast is ever present for Whitney Page and Louise, but support is another thing entirely. On campus the lower social class language, attitudes, modes of politeness, dress, behaviors, and values tend to be stigmatized and negatively sanctioned through interpersonal actions. "Look at what she's wearing," "You like that kind of food?" and "That's so middle class" are typical negative statements. Stigmatized forms of underclass behaviors are actively, not passively, sanctioned. For example, lower social class students are told in classes that their speech patterns and writing are wrong and their in-class behaviors are impolite. Seen through a multicultural lens, lower social class students' speech patterns, writing, and classroom behavior are different, nonnormative, and deviant. Those in the majority class culture who see themselves as the keepers of standards for their social class see these as wrong and deserving of negative sanctions.

Support, or even tolerance, for underclass social class norms, especially language norms, is lacking on campus. Lower social class dialects are stigmatized when students are taught prestige dialects, or "roper English." Classroom behaviors that may be normative in lower social classes are similarly stigmatized in classrooms; turn taking, hand raising, and polite forms of address from an upper-class perspective are normative in classes.

## Class passing

Thomas was a working-class first-generation student and is now a professor of sociology at TFSU that has only about 20% first-generation students. TFSU faculty have a strong tradition of publishing. The pressure on Tom to fit in in his attributed social class identity is tremendous. He manages his attributed social class carefully. His PhD is from one of the most prestigious programs in the nation, and his undergraduate degree is from a high-prestige state school. His academic work is in the area of public opinion, and his publication record is excellent. He is active in his national organization and has never been chair of any national committee. He is sociable and never hosts parties at his house. He is well dressed in classic fashion and long sleeves cover his tattoos. His office is neat, and the art on his walls are reproductions of classic paintings. His language is careful and measured, and his accent is neutral. No immediate cues tell his friends and colleagues about his precollege days. He provides no behavioral cues or behavioral traces that reflect his social class of origin. Tom's denial of his poverty-class roots is the precursor of stress, anxiety, depression, health problems, and various other ailments and life difficulties.

Being class outed is the fear that drives *class passing*, which is acting like the majority class even though you are not a member. This is the consequence of Louise's internalizing the negative stereotypes associated with her social class of origin. In a cartoon one man is flapping his arms and actually flying. The other man in the cartoon comments, "I don't care what you can do, you went to a state college."

Timothy is a professor at "Access State University," which has about 50% first-generation students. He has embraced his working-class origins in his work as a sociologist. He dresses comfortably, rarely wears a tie, and never wears a suit. His writing reflects the prestige U.S. English dialect, but his spoken language is that of his social class of origin, albeit with an educated vocabulary. Timothy is known around campus for his classed behaviors. His confrontational style is at odds with the collaboration valued in faculty governance, so he is not invited to participate on campus committees. His beer drinking in working-class bars does not provide him with opportunities to build social capital with his faculty colleagues. Timothy's publication record is excellent, and this record is the only thing that has allowed him to move up in faculty rank. Timothy originally expected accommodation from campus for his tastes, fashion, and speech patterns, and over time he came to realize that he had to go along to get along. His rejection of his attributed social class has made him an outcast on campus. His friends come from the working classes and, while initially suspicious of him because of his occupation and education, include Timothy in their activities. Timothy's lack of social attachments on campus and lack of fit with his working-class friends can easily lead to stress, anxiety, depression, and other problems brought on by social isolation.

## Class as role

Goffman (1959) wrote about our interpersonal cues and roles. Attributed social class can be seen as assigning people to social roles. Currently social class can be seen as assigning oneself to a role. The roles are scripts and costumes and set decoration that all depend on how we visualize the role. Roles are actions and behaviors. Actors act a role; they aren't passive in a role. Actors have the advantage of a script, direction, other actors following the same script, a stage, lighting, and all the trappings of theater.

Gender is an enacted role. Sex is passive; it exists if I am asleep or awake. The gender socialization process is about learning the role of male or female. The gender maturity process is about learning the role of mature manhood and mature womanhood. Gender bending is about performing the wrong lines in the play, about acting in the wrong way, about wearing the wrong costume. Class is an enacted role, and class socialization is a process of learning that social class role. Culture is an enacted role. Achieving cultural competence in a second culture is the process of learning a second role. Achieving competence in a second class is the process of learning a second role.

## Summary

The development of a conscious and integrated social class identity is a complex process similar to the conscious and integrated gender identity, ethnic identity, spiritual identity, sexual preference identity, or familial relationship identity. The starting point is awareness, and the ending point is integration. Experiences with other people on campus help students from the nonmajority class to become aware of class identity readily and often. Experiences with other people on campus hinder students from the majority class to become aware of class identity leading to a denial of class and a denial of the importance of class on campus.

## Experience

Listen. Take the time to make the effort to seek out people from a social class of origin other than yours and listen to them. Discover what the class-based experiences were for them. What is it like to be a first-generation student on your campus? What is it like to be a second- or third-generation student on your campus? Which faculty were first-generation students, which were second, which are second-generation professors? Which administrators were first-generation students, which were second, which are second-generation campus administrators? Ask them about their experiences on campus, and ask them about their experiences in high school.

How do we best begin a conversation about class? Just begin. "Hey, Bob, I've been reading this book about social class on campus—it's required for one of my classes—and the author says we all need to have a conversation about social class. I'm not sure even what to ask people. My parents both went to school here, so I am a second-generation college student, so this campus feels familiar to me. Are you a second-generation student like me? What was your first week on campus like?"

Explore what you believe about class and listen to what others believe about class. Class is a social construct rather than a set of truths, so articulating this social construct is the best place to start. Your experience is your experience and will be quite different from someone else's experience. That does not make all opinions equal. Nor is it true that minority class members know all about majority class members. Listening to others is the end of your denial of class differences and the beginning of your awareness, knowledge, and skill in working with class.

## Reflection question

How will knowing more about social class identity help you in relationships with people from other social class groups?

## Discussion questions

Is there really such a thing as social class identity?

Does it diminish the importance of discussions about gender identity and ethnic identity to include discussions of social class identity?

When you are meeting new people, for example, during your first few hours at college, are you more aware of your gender, your ethnicity, or your class?

Are you more sensitive to the social class cues, symbols, and status of people of higher social class than yours or lower social class than yours?

How is social class identity similar to or different from gender identity?

How is social class identity similar to or different from ethnic identity?

How is social class identity similar to or different from religious identity?

Have you ever felt you have moved up or down in social class?

How do you adjust your language and manners in different situations, like lunch with your friends or a formal dinner?

# CHAPTER 5

# *The Majority Class Student Experience of Class on Campus*

## Choosing how we name classes

A FEW WORDS about the power of naming classes are important. This chapter could have been titled "The Middle-Class Student on the Middle-Class Campus," but that would perpetuate inaccurate ideas of who is in the middle class and what campuses are like. This chapter could have been called "The Middle-Class Student Inexperience of Class on Campus," which is accurate but takes a while to explain. The term *middle class* is ambiguous and is often used without regard for boundaries, definitions, and comparison groups. This chapter has the stories of Misty from the majority class on campus, Ursula, and Eleanor. The next chapter deals with the college stories of Whitney Page and Louise.

The majority of students on nearly every four-year campus are second-, third-, or fourth-generation students, and their parents both work. From a U.S. demographic perspective these students come from families with educations, which puts them in the upper 29% of the population in educational attainment, and most likely in the top 20% for parental occupational prestige, and in the top 20% for parental income. Demographically, these students come from families that are in the upper 20% for income and education, which is hardly in the middle of any class group. All students are above average given the right comparison group. Given the right comparison group, you can be middle class with an income of $250,000 a year. The majority class for the students on any campus is a matter of student demographics, which tell us that students in the majority campus class are second generation, that they are the children of college-educated parents. The majority class on campus are the children of the 29% who are the most well-educated people in the United States.

The experiences of Ursula at a Seven Sisters college are the experiences of resonance, of fit. The experiences of Misty at TFSU, which has 20% first-generation students, are the experiences of resonance, of fit. The experiences of Louise at a community college that has 70% first-generation students are the experiences of resonance, of fit. Whitney Page and Eleanor don't fit easily on any campus. Accommodations are made for them, more so for Eleanor than for Whitney Page, but their differences, their contrast to the campus majority social class, their dissonance from the majority campus class culture, their lack of fit on campus are a daily experience for each of them.

When social class contrast is high students will mark, notice, and regard social class on campus. For Whitney Page and Louise at TFSU, social class contrast is immediately noticeable. For Misty at TFSU, social class contrast is so low it's unnoticeable. Class on campus for Misty is exactly the same as class at home and at high school. For Ursula contrast is moderate, and for Eleanor contrast is high.

## Misty goes to college

It is difficult not to portray Misty as a cartoon character. She is described here as an example of one kind of majority student, albeit extreme in her insensitivity to class. Her story is written to illustrate key issues for a majority class student on a majority campus. The class clue phone had not rung for Misty before college, and even when it rang during college, she didn't answer it. There are many ways to be a third-generation student with two parents who work. The roommates in these stories reflect other women in the middle class from backgrounds similar to Misty's and are presented as different ways students from similar backgrounds can act out their class role.

Misty has always been Mommy and Daddy's princess, and she had an especially close relationship with her mother. She had been treated with deference at home and had continually been told how good she was, how smart she was, and how special she was. This continual reinforcement had shaped Misty's worldview. She simply deserved things. Hard work had nothing to do with getting what she wanted. While not clinically narcissistic, Misty was close to being so. At home she never shared a room, a toy, clothing, a phone, a car, nothing. There had always been money for what she wanted, and her spending had not been monitored closely. Misty considers herself upper class and wants to belong to Eleanor's world without any real understanding of how the world of wealth is different. As a senior in high school she went on spring break with some high school friends and met some students from TFSU. Misty and several of her friends decided to go to TFSU. She had heard a lot about the campus sports teams and about events on campus, and all of her friends agreed that it is a good school. While Misty was very smart and academically talented, Ursula and Louise would describe Misty as shallow and "all about looking good."

Misty was assigned Michelle as a roommate, and the two women knew each other from an encounter at spring break and from an on-campus party the previous spring. Michelle is the child of college-educated parents, she is smart and academically accomplished. The two women spend the summer coordinating their dorm room, settling on who brings the TV, who brings the DVD player, and what their colors will be for the first semester. Misty bought a new Mac laptop because she thinks they are cute and likes the colors and because her friends thought they are cool (read prestige). Each of the women had her own mini refrigerator because "We just can't share that." Her family caravaned to campus, where her parents were legacy students. Misty rode with her mother while her brother and father traveled in the family SUV. Her father and brother carried everything into her room so Misty's outfit, hair, and nails didn't get mussed. Her roommate,

Michelle, and family arrived similarly, and the families left for home once the boxes were in the room.

Unpacking for the two women was an event and a contest. Misty's four Prada bags, two for fall and winter and two for eveningwear, made her the fashion winner. Having achieved material dominance Misty felt good about herself. After two days on campus the roommates took a weekend trip to Chicago because "no one really wants to shop locally." They made their fashion adjustments to fit in on campus and were back on Sunday evening ready for class on Monday. The women took the time to find a good nail salon, a good hair salon, a good tanning salon, and a good makeup supply counter. They brought this information back to the women on their floor, complained about how horrible all of the other salons are and that their salons were the best and most expensive. Some of the women on their floor were impressed, and some were not.

Fall semester brought sorority rush, and Misty's mother phoned every day with dress and presentation advice so Misty could join the same sorority her mother had joined. Misty's classes were not that challenging, and her time was spent on consuming. Shopping, manicures/pedicures, waxing, tanning, hair, and makeup occupied a lot of time. Misty was high maintenance. She was living the life she imagined Eleanor lived, the life represented in magazines targeting young women like Misty. Misty had an outfit for every occasion and shopped in her exercise clothes; for Misty, shopping was her exercise. She had a credit card from home and knew how much she could spend before getting a call from Mom. Dating was a part of college life for Misty, but she mostly saw men as providers to buy her things or to give her an entrance to prestigious social circles. Men thought of Misty as high-prestige arm candy.

On dates, in the hallways, and in her residence hall, Misty talked about Misty. She used phrases like "She is so middle class" to describe women she didn't like. Misty couldn't understand why women on her floor who ignored her or who openly didn't like her didn't want to be like her. She was outspokenly critical of others and usually made class statements about people. During sorority rush she was equally outspoken. Her chosen chapter almost didn't accept her. Some other sororities were composed almost entirely of Misty clones, but they weren't the cool (read prestige) sororities for Misty. She was rushed by two of them but rejected them quickly based on pressure from her mother. The women on the standards committee in the sorority Misty joined prepared themselves for a session with Misty about her negative attitude and about her disparaging remarks about other women. Misty did well academically during the fall and participated in her classes. She asked each professor if she could take the final early because her family had made plans that couldn't be changed. She didn't tell the professors that the plans were a ski vacation in Vail, Colorado.

At the end of her first year Misty was a full member of her sorority, and her circle of friends was limited to her sisters. She dated a few men but was not in a serious relationship. Misty had not participated in any leadership workshops, had not joined any organizations other than her sorority, had not visited the health center, the career center, the counseling center, or the student activities center. Misty believed that any on-campus service was beneath her and was just not good enough. "If these people were any good they would be in private practice."

Michelle, Misty's roommate, decided to join student government her first semester and chose not to join a sorority. Michelle was invited to participate in leadership training because she showed promise as a leader. Michelle was in student government in high school and had had leadership training before, and she continued to move up in student government and became involved in a number of campus organizations, rising eventually to sit on the executive committee of student government as a senior. By the time Michelle was a senior she had participated in seven leadership workshops sponsored by TFSU. The rich got richer.

Misty did well as a business major, and the campus encounters she had with gender, ethnicity, and class didn't affect her much. Misty continued to present herself well through her purchases and never gave in to self-reflection. She experienced periods of depression and loneliness, but she had learned to manage them with retail therapy. She did not recognize that her judgmental ways kept people away from her. She did not recognize a slowly growing insecurity and covered all her symptoms with more retail therapy. The encounters that challenged her privilege grew in number but not in effect. Professors in upper-level classes expected her to perform and turn papers in on time and gave her no special favors. The standards committee in her sorority met with her about her superior attitude, and Misty learned to change her behaviors in the sorority context. Her sociology class required community service, and when she was bagging groceries for the poor she noticed an item that she was used to eating and commented, "These people get to eat this?" not recognizing that it was donated because it was near its expiration date.

At 25 years old, working full-time at a job she considered beneath her—she deserved to start at the manager's level after all—she met George, who was not the man of her dreams, was not from a prestige class, didn't dress in prestige fashion clothing, but she really liked him. Trying to reconcile her emotional attachment to George with her fantasy partner and fantasy life in Eleanor's world was difficult and led finally to reflection and introspection. In a drunken evening all of her posturing, fashion role, sorority relationships, hopes, and dreams came tumbling out, and George still saw someone he liked. This transformation may not have occurred without her encounter experiences in college, but George did remind her of some of her professors who were not in the least impressed with her appearance.

I am indebted to Heather Miklosek and Stephanie Squires for their help in writing Misty's story.

## So what?

Misty's campus experiences maintain her class bubble. She has remained gender isolated, ethnically isolated, and class isolated in spite of having experiences with diverse students. The university provides Misty with a playground much like her home and her high school. The Misty character has been written to be resistant to the experiences that would help her encounter class, to cause dissonance in her life that leads to awareness. Misty has spent time easily taking advantage of those campus experiences that reinforce class, that confirm class, that cause her class resonance. Misty is described here as one possible example of the majority class on campus. There are many others.

TFSU's campus is made for Misty. The organizations, campus structures, language, food, and fashion are all confirmation experiences for Misty's idea of class. She does not have the advantage of class contrast that Whitney Page and Louise have. She has not grown up class conscious as have Ursula and Eleanor. Interpersonally Misty represents what many students on campus want to be, to have the appearance of the prestige class, to have the appearance of sophistication.

## Ursula goes to college

Ursula went to a highly selective Seven Sisters college where she was given a leadership scholarship. While her parents paid for Ursula's college tuition, room, board, fees, and books, she was expected to work while she was on campus. Ursula will eventually inherit money but doesn't have a trust fund. While she didn't need to worry about educational expenses, her parents and family expected her to earn her own way in the world.

Social class contrast is the heart of Whitney Page's and Louise's campus experiences. Lack of social class contrast, or college as a class confirmation experience, is the heart of Misty's story. The primary difference between Misty and Ursula is in the cultural capital, the social capital, the life experiences, and the skills they each bring to campus. Ursula went to college very class aware because of her experiences living around the world. To paraphrase the Educational Testing Service's (2007) statement on the relationship between money and test scores, it's not the money, it's the experiences that money provides.

The all-women's residential campus of about 2,000 students was situated in a small New England town with a full array of majors. About 30% of the students were international or non–European American. Many students had grants because they had high grades and SAT scores and came from low-income families. The campus administrators worked hard to maintain as much diversity as possible within the limits of the admissions criteria.

On move-in day Ursula arrived on campus with her mother. Because she had been on campus four times as part of her college selection process she knew her way around, and they drove directly to her residence hall. The residential adviser (RA) knew Ursula by e-mail from contacting her over the summer, and Ursula had been in contact with her roommate over the summer to negotiate who was bringing what. After the boxes and bags were placed in the room, Mom left and the RA took Ursula up and down the hall for introductions.

Ursula's roommate, Nadia, showed up by herself, and the two women chatted like old friends because they both had excellent social skills and because they had been chatting online all summer. At dinnertime the RA gathered the women and everyone went to the dining hall. After dinner the RA brought everyone into the lounge for a floor meeting and went over questions and basic information about living on campus. At 9:00 P.M. all the RAs gathered everyone to go downstairs for a hall meeting.

The next day every student met with her adviser in groups, usually 10 women to an adviser, and class schedules were developed, majors were discussed, and social capital was built. Each student was asked to bring a schedule back to her adviser the next day for a one-on-one conference. After lunch the RA sent small groups of women off on a campus tour with a sophomore, and every student signed up for a library orientation session. During the day Ursula went into every building and began to hear some of the stories about buildings and alumnae. Her group met a campus police officer on his Segway, and Ursula noticed that the officer was meeting every group of women walking around campus that day. When her group of students returned to their residence hall, two students from the campus information technology office were in the lobby asking if anyone needed help getting her computer set up.

Ursula's experiences in classes were what she had expected. A typical class had a mix of lecture and discussion, many papers were assigned, and the exams were mostly essay. She was an active participant in the discussions during class time, and she chatted with the professor after class. Ursula decided to try out for the crew team, and she was warmly welcomed even though she had never participated in athletics in high school. Many of the other rowers were experienced, but some were first timers. Because of the long hours of training, Ursula learned to manage her time carefully. Her relationship with Nadia grew, and while each woman had different social and academic interests they made sure to eat dinner together a few times each week. Ursula, always an early riser, got to know the breakfast cooks and servers and developed a wide circle of friends on campus that crossed all boundaries. She joined a religious student group, a vegetarian student group, and a political action student group in which she became treasurer.

During the fall semester Ursula went to the counseling center to work on issues of stress and anxiety because she felt overwhelmed by her busy schedule and because she felt the pressure of family expectation for her performance in college. Her parents had been careful not to pressure Ursula to go into any particular major or line of work, but they expected her to succeed academically at whatever she did. Because almost everyone in her family was a professional of some sort she felt a lot of pressure to choose a professional major her first semester. This was not her first experience in counseling for stress and anxiety.

During the spring semester Ursula got a job on campus entering data for a faculty research project and used the money for trips with friends to Boston and New York since her parents provided only basic support. In March Ursula applied for an RA position, in part because it came with a single room and a cash stipend, and she was selected. Nadia had declared a computer science major and elected to move into a residence hall with many of the other women in her major.

Going home at the end of the semester was a time for rest and renewing family ties. Her parents and relatives were very interested in her experiences on campus and were very encouraging of her out-of-class activities, social and organizational. Talking about classes, books, ideas, professors, and other students was a natural conversation, and everyone had something to contribute. By the end of her first year Ursula had visited the counseling center, the career center, the math tutoring center, the health center, and had participated in two leadership training workshops sponsored by Student Activities. Ursula had sought out each of these experiences for herself. Over the summer, Ursula kept in touch with her friends through e-mail and did volunteer work in town.

Her second year was equally eventful even though she was no longer rowing crew. She declared majors in anthropology and political science and took a Spanish class to keep herself fluent. She continued to be politically active and spent most of her time on academic work. Her group of friends included people from her organizations, crew, her major, and several of the students from countries where she had lived. One of her favorite things to do was to seek out ethnic food restaurants with someone from that ethnic group. She worked with a faculty member on her research and spent some time with the family of the director of the career center who knew her father from professional activities. Ursula's junior year was spent in Scotland, and during her senior year she was head resident for her residence hall. After graduation she pursued paid and unpaid internships before starting law school with the career goal of working in social justice advocacy.

## So what?

Ursula's experience on campus is primarily about her taking advantage of what was available. Ursula was keenly aware that she was preparing herself for a career, creating a package of knowledge and experience. Her campus administrators worked to include diversity of every sort in the student body, to provide out-of-class experiences for students, to orient students to the campus and campus culture. Even though most of the women at Ursula's school arrived with social and cultural capital, the people conducting orientation realized these women didn't have cultural and social capital related to that campus. Ursula did mark the differences among the women, faculty, and staff on her campus because she grew up sensitized to differences. Ursula worked hard to cross the divide between groups, across class boundaries, religious boundaries, and national and ethnic boundaries. In reality there were students like Louise and Misty on this highly selective campus. Ursula had students in her classes who didn't mark difference and who felt entitled to be on that campus because of their family's social and economic standing. Ursula did not seek them out for conversation or friendship.

## Eleanor's story

Zweig (2000) notes in *The Working Class Majority* that there is a very small group of people who control most of the wealth in the United

States. Members of this group are whom people usually think of as the upper class. Members of this group are different from other people. However powerful they may be, they are few and subject to endless fascination. On a small number of highly selective campuses, these are important people. On the other 2,200 public and private not-for-profit four-year campuses, these people are irrelevant because of their small number.

This is the group that has old money, which means its members don't work for a living other than serving on boards and supervising their money managers. Some members of this elite class belong to the genteel poor, families that used to have old money that is now gone. Members of these genteel poor families have culture and connections but not wealth. The new rich, the gauche, those who work, or those who just have money but don't have the social capital are not members of this elite class. The new rich don't count as members of the elite class. "They're not rich; they just have money." The new rich are celebrities, people who appear in the news, on television, or in films, and the newly technowealthy. Even among the new rich there is a hierarchy. "Which Gulfstream do you fly?" is a question for the newly wealthy who still measure their status by their signs of wealth, their positional goods.

Casting Eleanor as a daughter from a family with wealth provides a different view of social class contrast and a brief look into this small group of people. For the elite wealthy, economic capital is assumed, cultural capital is slowly and continually accreted, and social capital is the primary source of interest that creates a network of social obligations that occupy a great deal of time. The children of the elite are not spoiled and not indulged. Much is expected of these children, and even though they will never work, they will contribute to society in meaningful ways.

Eleanor and all her friends are a small minority on any campus, so why include them in this chapter on majority class? Ursula and Eleanor come from a class that many others on campus aspire to. Ursula's urbane worldliness, massive cultural capital, and enviable social skills make her the poster child for those pursuing college to enter a profession. Eleanor comes from wealth, and the reality of her life on campus should be explored. The other reason to include Eleanor is to provide an accurate portrayal of this small group. Without it, readers would complain because this wealth group was not mentioned.

Eleanor lived in a major eastern city where her family had lived for years. Her mother's family and her father's family had been wealthy by U.S. standards for a long time. Her father served on the board of a prestigious law firm and on the boards of several hospitals, and he oversaw the family's business interests. Eleanor's mother was an equal partner in major decisions about their financial well-being. Her mother was always busy because running an elite-class family is a full-time job. She sat on several music and art boards, managed the events for several charities, scheduled and planned family gatherings, managed the household staff, managed all the residences, managed all the family's many social obligations, and kept contacts with the myriad essential people in her family's life.

Eleanor was raised by nannies and was mostly a latchkey child because her parents were very busy. She went to private day school through eighth grade and then went to a private boarding school in New England and was accepted into an Ivy League/Seven Sisters college. She was fairly certain that she was admitted because of her academic record, not because of her social class. She was aware of the affirmative action for the elite wealthy and the special favors she was prone to receive. While it bothered her and seemed a burden sometimes, people gave her privilege in large measures.

Eleanor arrived at college in her own car and unpacked her things herself. Her mother and aunts had given her a list of daughters to make contact with to stay connected. Each of these daughters also had been given Eleanor's name by their mothers and aunts. This network carried with it social obligations that take a great deal of time. These duties encroached on her study and activity time. The direct pressure from her mother for social contacts caused Eleanor a great deal of stress and anxiety. Eleanor's roommate, Bettina, was much like Ursula, well-traveled, good cultural capital, physician parents, and wealthy from a certain perspective but having little money from Eleanor's perspective. For Eleanor this class contrast with her roommate was a problem because she was never sure if people befriended her because of her social position or because they genuinely liked her. Fortunately, Bettina was not particularly impressed with Eleanor's social standing, and they got along well.

The fall passed in idyllic New England splendor. Eleanor rowed crew, as she did at boarding school, and when her parents donated money for a pair of carbon fiber oars nothing was said to Eleanor by anyone on the team or by the coaches. Her social obligations ate up a lot of time, and her mother checked in regularly. On a visit to campus Eleanor's mother invited Bettina to a formal affair in New York City in October that was mandatory for Eleanor. Bettina could not possibly afford the gown necessary for the gathering, so before Bettina could object or make excuses not to attend, Eleanor's mother said casually, "We'll get you something nice for the party when you come to the city." With that comment it was settled that Bettina would attend the gathering and stay at Eleanor's family's apartment at Beekman Place. The gathering turned out to be a formal ball featuring most of the social and political elite in New York City and Boston. Bettina had a wonderful time but found talking with people a chore because the primary topic was who was where and doing what. Bettina found substantive conversation, specific conversation about science, culture, art, or academic topics, lacking, as though it were vulgar to talk specifics about any topic.

The second semester Eleanor took two English classes, and a few weeks into the semester the chair of the English department asked her to tea. The conversation centered around Eleanor's experiences on campus, and the chair quietly probed for any sources of dissatisfaction, disaffection, or discomfort. This pattern of being invited to tea or to dinner by faculty and administrators lasted throughout her college experience and was part of her web of required social obligations. Eleanor was aware that her parents gave money to the college, and there was a campus building with her family name on it from a few generations ago. One time on campus she was walking with Bettina when someone said, "Hey, is that your building?" pointing to the one given to the college by a great-uncle. This was one of the few times that Bettina saw Eleanor uncomfortably embarrassed. To maintain her own social contacts Eleanor joined a private dining club. Even though these exclusive clubs were banned on campus, they were an institutionalized part of Eleanor's experiences.

Over the summer between her first and second year Eleanor took an unpaid internship working with autistic children. The arrangements were made through her parents' contacts. Even though she could have gotten the internship on her own, the family network, the web of obligations and relationships, was used. The internship was unpaid because Eleanor had always heard the family dictum, "Never take a job from someone who needs it." After her junior year she spent an internship in the old masters' section of an upscale art auction house.

Throughout her college years Eleanor saw a therapist to manage the stress and anxiety of meeting the academic requirements and the social obligations. In her classes she was graded using the same standards as all other students. Members of the campus accommodated Eleanor in many ways, and she received special treatment in nearly every way except for grades. Other than Bettina, Eleanor's friends were those in her social circle. Her general paranoia about relationships and about being exploited was always a background feature in any relationship. As the daughters of family friends came to campus each fall, Eleanor was obliged to see them all and to maintain the connections of the social fabric of her life. Even though she liked her science classes, her family discouraged her from pursuing science or medicine as a major or a career. Since the man she met at the auction house did not work out as a potential husband, Eleanor was encouraged to go to law school even though no one expected her to work. Finding the right husband was her ultimate job.

Eleanor graduated cum laude and went to an Ivy League law school. During her first year at the school her parents had several social gatherings and invited substantial numbers of single men and women from her social circle. The none-too-subtle message was that these gatherings contained the approved catalog of available mates for those in attendance. Eleanor found a suitable man (similar social standing, well educated, Ivy League MBA, and an internship with the board of a Fortune 100 company) at one of these gatherings, and they got married after she finished law school. She worked for two years in an upscale law firm owned by family friends, but only put in 30 hours per week because of her ongoing social obligations. Eleanor was an excellent attorney and was sought out by clients for her social connections and her legal abilities.

College was another obligation in Eleanor's life and had had little effect on her felt social class. In many ways the contrast between her social class of origin and the campus social class, typified by Bettina, has been managed by the social obligations and rituals that reinforce her way of life. Eleanor's social class has been layered on top of the campus social class.

I am indebted to Margaret Freebush Peabody-Saltonstall (not her real name) for a view into Eleanor's world.

## So what?

Stars always influence campus structures, organization, the constructed campus climate, and interpersonal interactions. Eleanor and her social circle are important to her campus for finance and perceived prestige. "Well, you know, the Peabody family has always gone here, and they recently gave us a new building." The campus foundation office is the primary structural component of an institution charged with attending to the needs of the elite upper-class students. The office staff sees to it that Eleanor gets invited to appropriate social gatherings and makes sure that she gets invitations to tea and dinner at faculty homes. The staff in the foundation office even reviewed her roommate assignment. While Whitney Page, Louise, Misty, and Ursula are expected to assimilate to campus, Eleanor and her friends are accommodated.

## Marking class on campus

Why is the majority class student experience unmarked? Members of the campus community normalize the majority class, and most members of TFSU aspire to be normal, to be like Misty, to behave according to the norms of her social class. Misty's normalization leads to negative sanctions for Whitney Page and Louise. The consequence of being in

the majority class is that it makes awareness of class much more difficult. For Misty the class awareness clue phone has not rung. She meets
people from different groups every day, but her encounter with class,
her awareness of class, is minimized to the extent that her class is normalized. For Louise the class clue phone rang the first day she was on
campus. For Ursula and Eleanor the class clue phone rang years before
college. For Misty the class clue phone has been drowned out in a sea
of sameness, of normalized class homogeneity on TFSU campus.

Many things happen to many students on campus. Astin's (1993)
model for assessing the student experience includes inputs, environments, and outcomes. This model is a good tool for understanding
students from multiple social classes. Using this model we can view
Whitney Page, Louise, Misty, Ursula, and Eleanor as inputs to campus.
We can view the majority social class culture as the environment. We
can view the outcomes as social class awareness, identity, graduation,
academic success, social success, and so forth. Students from different
social class groups move through different paths on campus. Whitney
Page will have different friends, rise to a different level of leadership,
and have a different collection of experiences in the college environment, and this will lead to different outcomes. Louise will have different friends, rise to a different level of leadership, and have a different
collection of experiences in the college environment, and this will lead
to different outcomes. You get the picture: Birds of a feather . . .

In the film adaptation of Steinbeck's *Cannery Row* (Ward, 1982) the
last line after the tumult of the film is spoken by the narrator, John
Huston: "Things were finally back to normal on Cannery Row. Once
more the world was spinning in greased grooves." The greased grooves
at TFSU belong to Misty's world. The greased grooves at the Seven
Sisters world belong to Ursula. Louise's experience on any campus is
marked by contrast; she has no beaten path, no greased grooves. Even
on an open-access state school campus, Whitney Page and Louise will
have trouble. Even though that campus might be 50% first-generation
incoming students, the other students and especially the faculty generate a campus majority social class that is not consistent with Louise's
social class of origin. Ursula's experience is unmarked, and she is
expected to have no problems because of her resources. Whitney Page's

and Louise's experiences are marked, and we hope that they will do well, somehow. Eleanor's experience on campus is marked by her social and economic wealth and members of the campus community accommodate her.

## The reproduction of class

Bourdieu (1986) writes about the reproduction of social class through social institutions. This reproduction has structural and interpersonal agency components. The college organizational structures and patterns of interpersonal relations that are familiar to Misty, Ursula, and Eleanor and unfamiliar to Whitney Page and Louise are one means by which social class is reproduced. Misty, Ursula, and Eleanor come to campus knowing how to use the system, and through the agency of their professors, RAs, student activities staff, advisers, support staff, and even cafeteria staff, social class is reproduced by advantaging one group and disadvantaging another.

The agent in class reproduction, social class contrast, and social class socialization is people. The agent is you. The agent is me. The agents are Whitney Page, Louise, Misty, Ursula, and Eleanor. The agent is each of us. The agent is our collective coevolution of classed campus norms. The agent is not us; the agent is each of us individually. If we suggest that the agent is an "us" or a "them," the role of the individual in the process of class discrimination and reproduction is diminished. It is far more pleasing to think about policies and the actions of large numbers of people than to think about our own actions. Thinking in the abstract is a way of absolving each of us of the responsibility for our actions. Classism and class reproduction are the result of individual actions. Class is interpersonal. Class is personal. Class is more than money.

Organizational structures and policies, such as the use of standardized tests in the college admissions decisions, are not the actions of "us" or "them" but are the actions of individuals. Each person who participates in using any standardized college admissions tests confirms the legitimacy of that process, and that means the test takers and the test users. Because that process is inherently discriminatory to individuals from economically disadvantaged backgrounds and those from groups that do not reflect prestige cultural capital knowledge and skills, each person who uses standardized test scores participates in this class-based discrimination. Look on the website for the ACT or SAT or GRE or LSAT or GMAT for information about the positive relationship between family income and test score. No one is trying to hide this information. There needs to be an ongoing cost (discrimination)-benefit (efficient and effective) analysis of the use of standardized testing. ACT, SAT, and GRE scores are about as well correlated with family income as they are with academic success. SAT and GRE scores only add about 15% to the certainty in predicting the academic success of students during their first year. To put it another way, standardized test scores and grades are an efficient and effective way to sort students during an admissions decision. Just because there is a relationship between family income and test scores does not de facto make it a bad or useless test.

## College as a confirmation experience: The world of accommodation

For Misty at TFSU and for Ursula at a Seven Sisters college, their experiences act as confirmation of their social class. It is difficult for majority class students on U.S. majority class campuses to experience the social class contrast that serves to create an awareness of class. How do you explain water to a fish? How do you explain Whiteness to a European American student on a majority European American campus? How do you explain class to a fifth-generation legacy student on a selective college campus who has lived in a class bubble of gated communities and private schools all his or her life? When we explain Whiteness or water or class to the majority class student who sees these as the way the world works, the student will note: "Of course student organizations all have presidents, vice presidents, secretaries, and treasurers. All organizations are like that." The student will not see organizational structures as a function of culture, or class, or ethnicity, or gender.

Awareness of the world we live in is difficult if we don't have contrast. The age-old question springs to mind: Can we know beauty without ugliness? Can we know light without dark? Can we know joy without sorrow? Can we become aware of gravity without experiencing weightlessness? When you lift a fish out of the water to experience air it gasps for air, collapses from the high gravity, and finds vision difficult. When you return the fish to water, if it could talk it might say: "I couldn't breathe or see and I was pressed down by some invisible force. Nothing was normal." Next time you go swimming take a moment to experience the world underwater, the fish's world. You can't see, you can't breathe, and gravity is turned off.

One can imagine the corollary. Imagine Misty participating in a college service-learning trip to rural Mexico. The rural Mexican rules of social interaction and symbolic interaction just don't apply to the European American suburban second-generation student context. On returning to her campus Misty reflects: "It was horrible. Everything was different. Nothing made sense. These people just didn't do anything right. It was definitely not normal." Given guidance and time to reflect perhaps Misty would have understood difference.

What if Misty had not gone on that trip? What happens when a student goes to a campus that provides little or no social class contrast? Is this like keeping a fish in water? What happens when Louise or Misty or Ursula goes to a college filled with people like her? Social class contrast is minimized because the student body is homogenized. Those few students who are from different class groups are socializing themselves and trying to class pass to fit in. The physical environment, the social environment, the institutional structures, and the interpersonal relationships all confirm Louise's, Misty's, and Ursula's ideas of normalcy of the environment, the structures, and interactions. Campus becomes a confirmation experience, reinforcing cultural norms and the normalcy of this culture. This heightens the abnormalcy of other cultures and classes.

The confirmation of class for Misty happens in many ways: through the normalization of language, fashion, social norms, social skills, organization and the distribution of power, and the constructed meaning of interactions among others. Normalization leads to entitlement, rightness, the affirmation of moral correctness, and a monoparadig-matic worldview reflecting a majority class view. The process of normalization can be seen from many perspectives, but the bias in this book is to view processes and events as the sum of interpersonal interactions. Consequently, a closer look at the confirmation of class and the campus member's roles in conforming class is needed. Wanting to be perceived as abnormal is why class minority students often try hard to fit in, to appear normal by becoming normal, by becoming like Misty and Ursula in every possible way.

## Campus class markers: Fashion

Dress and fashion are prominent features of any campus environment. Students, faculty, and staff make individual dress and fashion choices that in the aggregate constitute the campus dress and fashion norms, including subgroup norms. How students dress comes from a variety of social interactions and influences. Campus faculty and staff modeling is one source of influence. While students are unlikely to copy faculty and staff fashion literally, the formal or informal nature of faculty and staff dress will set a campus tone. Business students often dress differently than education students. Wearing obviously labeled fashions featuring brand names emblazoned across chests and rear ends is an obvious statement of belongingness. Wearing subtly labeled fashions is another obvious statement of belongingness. There is fashion and there is alternative or antifashion. There is prestige fashion (Prada) and there is antiprestige (plaid and camouflage) fashion. The reality is that fashion and prestige are close friends, but different people wear each style. Because certain patterns of dress and fashion are valued, other patterns of dress and fashion are devalued, creating a collection of negative sanctions for dressing out of the class norm. Misty and Ursula and Eleanor came to campus ready for success and able to afford wardrobe adjustments if they didn't quite fit in.

## Campus class markers: Language

Written language and spoken language have different places on campus. Both are interpersonally transmitted norms for class. Faculty and staff choices to use a prestige dialect in spoken English will create the norms of a prestige class and will devalue low-prestige varieties or dialects of English. Faculty demands that students use proper English, whatever that may be, are common. These demands leave out the uncomfortable discussion of who controls what gets called proper English. Misty, Ursula, and Eleanor, from their privileged upbringings, come to campus with the prestige dialect as their native language. They can read and write what people believe to be proper English but is really a prestige class variety of English. Whitney Page and Louise have many regional colloquialisms in their written and spoken language because their high schools focused on preparing students for the multiple-choice, high-stakes graduation exams rather than on language and writing for college.

The interaction between ethnicity and class is easy to spot when language comes into play on campus. Students from poor rural schools and poor urban schools come to campus with low-prestige dialects. If Louise is successful on campus and normalizes to the prestige dialect she will go home and be criticized for sounding uppity. Ethnic minority students who speak with a prestige dialect are often criticized by their peers as sounding too White. No one on campus will criticize Misty, Louise, or Ursula for sounding too White or too uppity, or for sounding like they are "getting above their raising."

## Campus class markers: Social interaction

Social interaction, like language and dress and fashion, is classed. Norms of prestige social interaction are very subtle, and Ursula comes to the highly selective campus already using prestige social interaction learned through her multinational and multicultural experiences in her family. Misty comes to campus monocultural, but her culture is the prestige culture, and she exhibits the patterns of social interaction that she learned at home from her parents who learned them in their professional lives. Talking with a professor after class is a comfortable social interaction for Misty, Ursula, and Eleanor. Those three women grew up dealing with their friends' parents and their parents' friends, learning the social dance steps of the managerial and professional class.

Because of the social interaction skills these students brought to campus, meeting other people is comfortable to them, and building new social networks to increase social capital is an everyday task. The assumption that everyone who matters—those who have power and resources—uses the same patterns of social interaction further reinforces the normalcy of these patterns. Is it any wonder that Misty, Ursula, and Eleanor get on well with their professors, advisers, and residence hall staff? Is there any question that student involvement, the central element of retention according to Tinto (1993), is related to social interaction skills?

There is a secret handshake among those with prestige social interaction skills. Stand, approach the other person, look him or her in the eye, smile, and introduce yourself if you are meeting for the first time or if the person may not recall your name, and give a firm handshake. This is a skill that is easily practiced but rarely employed.

## Campus class markers: Organizational structure

It rarely occurs to most people on campus that organizational structures have a classed history. The structure of formal organizations, from intramural teams to student organizations, reflects a classed notion of organization. The structure of formal organizations—president, vice president, secretary, treasurer, and other sundry officials—is so ingrained in the way we do business, in hierarchies, or in our work that we don't think of it as classed. Organizational structures are one of the ways college reproduces social class. Giving students the opportunity to practice work-related hierarchy role skills is a good thing. These formally articulated hierarchies come from a culture that values efficiency and clarity and clear assignments in the hierarchy. Higher up on the organizational hierarchy means more power, prestige, money, and class because your work role defines your social class in this system. On both ends of the class spectrum this association of person and work role breaks down. For many of us the work we do is part of our identity; for others in the poverty class and lower working

class as well as those in the nonworking elite class, identity and work
are separate.

## Campus class markers: Leadership

Leadership is a social experience, and the ways professionals in the campus community model leadership affect students' leadership skills. Bolman and Deal's (2008) frames provide four ways to look at leadership:
structural, relational, ideological, and political. Better leaders, they
assert, use multiple frames. The structural frame is the hierarchy frame
that students are taught in student organizations. The relational frame
is social capital and interpersonal skills that some students are taught
in leadership skills workshops. The ideological frame is rarely discussed
and even more rarely do we teach the skills needed to discuss this
frame. The political frame is based on social capital and the ability to
build coalitions, a skill largely ignored in leadership training, student
organizations, and college classrooms.

Kouzes and Posner (2003) assert that credibility is the key to leadership. The leader must be believable. Questioning the idea of credibility
foregrounds the idea of whom I find credible. Will I find someone who
speaks like Rambo credible, or like Tom and Ray Magliozzi (the *Car
Talk* brothers), or will I find someone credible who speaks authorita-
tively in a prestige dialect, like the presidents Franklin Roosevelt, John
Kennedy, and Barack Obama? The skill of seeming credible is learned
and is directly related to class.

College confirms the place in leadership for everyone on campus,
from stars to bit-part players. Whitney Page and Louise become bit-
part players on TFSU campus; they become nonmembers, not being
invited to join organizations that will help build interpersonal skills
and not being invited to leadership skill-building events. Misty finds a
place in a campus sorority and is never invited to take a leadership
position, largely because of her classist worldview and because her
roommate, Michelle, moves quickly up the leadership ladder. Ursula is
welcomed when she joins the crew team. She is welcomed when she
joins student organizations her second semester. Her peers find her

credible, and she is recruited to participate in leadership training experiences. Campus professionals don't recruit Eleanor into any student organization, student government, or any sports team; they respect her autonomy and are more than a little afraid of offending such a potentially powerful person.

## Campus class markers: Learning experiences

Classroom-based learning is structured in a specific way that can be viewed as class based. Ask yourself if you are more likely to have more lectures or more discussions at a prestigious, selective private campus. Baxter-Magolda's (2009) concept of self-authorship assumes a level of in-class interaction in which a student's points of view are valued and out-of-class reflections are part of these experiences. There is a class overtone in the attitude that students in classrooms are the recipients of received knowledge, which is quite different from the attitude that students are the cocreators of constructed knowledge. The student who has had the opportunity to cocreate constructed knowledge is far more likely to grow toward self-authorship than the student who sits in classrooms receiving knowledge from the sage on the stage. Who is more likely to become more completely self-authored, Whitney Page, Louise, Misty, Ursula, or Eleanor?

The style of teaching on each of these women's campuses will probably reflect the style evident in their high school classes. Whitney Page and Louise, coming from a lecture world in high school, find comfort in lecture formats at TFSU. They like not having to talk in class because they have no practice at it. College confirms their worldview and their place in the world. Misty is in large lecture classes that create the same familiar class bubble around her. Ursula and Eleanor, with their high school advanced placement classes, find seminar and discussion formats familiar when they go to college. They had written long papers in high school, and they knew how to read and follow a syllabus, how to determine what a professor really wants, and how and when to talk with the professor outside class. Their experiences at college confirm their place in the world as their having a valued point of view.

## Campus class markers: The physical campus

The inside and outside physical campus environment reflects an architecture selected by someone or some committee. Close your eyes and imagine the campus of one of the Ivy League/Seven Sisters schools Ursula and Eleanor attended. Your imagination and the architecture on these campuses will generally match. Gleaming new buildings spread among old ivy-covered halls named after well-known and internationally famous donors. Even those state college administrators who proclaim their campus to be an oxymoronic public ivy spend time and money on the physical campus to create and convey that image. Oddly enough, some of the Ivy League/Seven Sisters schools are physically shabby, and evidence of deferred maintenance is readily apparent.

Imagine for a moment a state college, an open-access college, where Whitney Page's and Louise's younger brothers may choose to go. The architecture is functional, the buildings are designed for use, there is no ivy, streets run through the campus, the classrooms are a little shabby—you get the picture. What the state built was for first-generation, second-class citizens. No resources were used for what were seen as frills for these students. There is little art, little decor, and the coffee shop serves powdered latte. The college physical plant is functional. Imagine for a minute the local branch of a community college. The physical plant is even more functional, efficient, and with minimal regard for aesthetics. High School High Community College features cinder-block walls, long hallways, and lockers.

Each of the physical plants confirms Whitney Page's, Louise's, Misty's, Ursula's, and Eleanor's place in the world. Visit the union buildings at the public ivy schools and you will see architecture, art, and decor that reflect the aspirational class of the students. Deconstructing the physical environments of state colleges is an exercise in understanding how members of the state legislature and government value the students at each campus. The campus buildings, classrooms, study spaces, art, decor, and meeting rooms are comfort food for your eyes if they are authentic to your social class of origin.

## Class passing

For the majority student on the majority campus, for Misty, class passing is invisible. Misty, who is all about appearance, doesn't notice the subtle cues from anyone who is passing for a different class. Louise and Whitney Page, all dressed up, could walk by Misty in the hallway, and Misty would not notice their class passing. Ursula and Eleanor could walk by Misty in the hallway, and Misty would not notice their class. Campus White trash parties are about dressing up, not about class passing. Antifashion is about dressing up, not about class passing.

The motivation for class passing is fitting in. For some people this could be about joining the majority, and for others fitting in could be about not wanting to stand out. Deviance from the norm is negatively sanctioned, so obvious signs of class deviance bring subtle and pointed sanctions. Not all students seek to class pass. Some underclass students will band together and reward each other for not fitting in, typically using fashion as a class group identity marker, wearing flannel or camouflage. Eleanor will seek to class pass by minimizing her observable class difference unless she is with others from the elite class.

## The monoculture campus

A great deal has been researched and written about the experiences of women in all-women's colleges, about the experiences of African Americans at historically Black colleges and universities (HBCUs), about the experiences of First Nations students at tribal colleges, and about the experiences of students at faith-based colleges. For most of these students the experiences are formative and positive. On an all-women's campus women are no longer negatively sanctioned for their work in math and science. For ethnic minority students or for First Nations students attending colleges serving these groups, authentic behaviors, music, and food are not scorned. For religious minorities at faith-based colleges, religious practices and beliefs are not marginalized. These are good things. For a majority student on a majority campus these same reinforcements are not a good thing.

## The dangers of being the majority

The most dangerous outcome of being a majority class student on a majority class campus is the constant reinforcement of the appropriateness and superiority of class-based norms, behaviors, dress, behavioral patterns, politeness, forms of social organization, rituals, and all other features of class. While this reinforcement is central to the positive experiences of women on an all-women's campus, the reinforcement on the majority social class campus is central and negative because of the lack of multiple class perspectives and class diversity. Homogeneity is the pattern on the majority culture campus. Homogeneity is the antithesis of heterogeneity and diversity in any form. Seen in this lens, the reaction against diversity is a reaction for homogeneity. The diversity wars seen in this light are class wars, as well as ethnic and gender wars.

## Experience

*Middle-class values* is a term often used but rarely defined. Spend an hour talking with members of the majority class on your campus and identify the values and beliefs they have in common. Start by describing their fashion, their taste in food and music, their attitude toward education—why they are in college—and their attitude toward campus groups like Goths, hipsters, art majors, and so forth who are perceived as outsiders by members of the majority culture.

# Reflection questions

In what ways are your attitudes, behaviors, and fashion, food, and music preferences different from those of people in the majority social class on your campus?

In what ways are your attitudes, behaviors, and fashion, food, and music preferences similar to those of people in the majority social class on your campus?

# Discussion questions

Is it fair to group people into a majority social class on campus?

Describe the majority social class students on your campus. What do they dress like, what do they do for fun, what is their major, what computer do they have, what do they have in their room, and so forth?

What should people on your campus do to help students assimilate and become like people in the majority social class on your campus? Or, should no one be expected to assimilate?

What do faculty believe about the economic wealth and cultural wealth of students on your campus?

What are some examples of class assumptions in the way your campus administrators conduct their business? For example, do extra activities cost extra money?

How is social class presented and portrayed on primetime TV shows, and how is this reflected in student dress, fashion, and behaviors on your campus?

How are the characters in popular TV shows relevant on your campus?

Are TV shows designed to show an upper-middle-class and an upper-class reality designed to get viewers to desire the objects and lifestyle portrayed?

Is there an equivalent to sexism and racism that is classism? What would be some examples of classism? What would be some classist jokes or language?

Who is a professor more likely to call on or have as a favorite, someone from the majority class on campus or someone from the minority class?

# CHAPTER 6

# The Minority Class Student Experience of Class on Campus

## The lower-class experience on campus

Two QUALIFIERS are important in this chapter. First, lower class, or underclass, is being used here to identify students who are in the lower 60% of U.S. 18-year-olds, using economic, educational, and occupational attainment as a metric for class. The term *lower class* is used here to contrast with the majority college-going U.S. population represented by Misty, Ursula, and Eleanor. These lower-class, underclass, poverty-class, or working-class students are not from the typical four-year college student population. Whitney Page and Louise are poster children for the successful underclass, which is how they have been described here. It is important to note there are many characteristics of the lower class, and Whitney Page and Louise reflect only two of them.

Second, this discussion is restricted to four-year colleges and universities. As students have different social classes of origin, campuses have different social class cultures that reflect their student and faculty demographic, their history, and their mission. A branch campus will generally have a lower social class culture than the main campus; a community college will generally have a lower social class culture than a four-year campus. Restricting the discussion to similar types of non-profit public and private campuses is a convenience. This simplicity and convenience does not mean that class issues are unimportant for a lower-class student at a community college.

## College as a conversion experience: The world of assimilation

We all have deep emotional responses to being out of our class's comfort zone. An example would be Whitney Page in a fine dining establishment. The full array of preset water, white wine, and red wine glasses; forks; knives; spoons; and tableware contrasts dramatically with her usual dinner table. Another example would be Eleanor's brother Matthew dressed in his tailor-made suit in a beer joint and pool hall called the Honey Pot. This dissonance between our current felt social class and our immediate situation needs to be resolved. The easy resolution is to flee the scene, leave the restaurant, leave the bar and pool hall, or quit college. Whitney Page and Louise each resolved to come to campus to stay, but many experiences will make them consider the fleeing option. In our stories they muster the strength and support to stay. Unfortunately, campus faculty and staff don't provide appropriate support or help them find their strengths. Sadly, many women and men find themselves at a point where they decide not to continue college because of this lack of support.

Social class contrast, resulting from encounter experiences, is a central theme in the literature on students from the underclasses who come to campus. Fitting in, getting by, and class passing are the typical experiences of students experiencing social class contrast. Underclass students have similar encounter experiences to ethnic minority students on predominantly White campuses in that there is constant contrast and conflict.

## Whitney Page's story

Whitney Page came from a world of jobs, not of careers. Family members and friends have had a series of hourly wage jobs, and any job advancement they have experienced involved moving up to another level of an hourly wage job or moving to a new hourly wage job in a different company. Her high school guidance counselor was little help in preparing Whitney Page for college. She was not automatically enrolled in the college preparation program in her school, and when Whitney Page asked the guidance counselor about college she was only given information on the local community college. College was never emphasized because she went to school in a low-income neighborhood. She didn't know what to ask about college, and she didn't know what she needed to know about college.

For Whitney Page college was not about the on-campus experience, involvement, culture, social learning, leadership workshops, art openings, concerts, student organizations, and all that Misty, Ursula, and Eleanor took for granted. College for Whitney Page was not about packaging and positioning herself for the right job and career or preparing for graduate school. For Whitney Page college was about classes, a degree, and getting a better job.

Whitney Page applied to two state colleges, but her guidance counselor tried to dissuade her from going to college because it wasn't for "people like her." She applied for financial aid with her minister's help, and because he went to TFSU he took her on a campus visit that centered on a meeting with people in the financial aid office. She was very surprised to be offered a scholarship because of her SAT scores and grades; she was unaware that such scholarships existed. Her scholarship and financial aid offer at TFSU provided her with enough money to cover all college, book, and on-campus living expenses if she stuck to a tight budget. There was no extra money unless she got a job, so college experiences that cost money were not on her agenda. Because she qualified for the work-study program, she was able to find a job on campus. Because she had a scholarship and because one of her friends from high school went to TFSU, Whitney Page decided that was the place for her.

On move-in day her minister drove her to campus because her mother couldn't get a day off work. Whitney Page came to campus with one suitcase of clothing, some new pens and notebooks, and not much else. A single trip from the car was all it took to bring her things into the room, and after a tearful good-bye her minister left for home. Alone in the room Whitney Page was terrified and didn't have any idea what to do next. Because TFSU is only 25% first-generation students, chances were good that she would have a legacy as a roommate, and sure enough, Willow, her new roommate, showed up with her family. Everyone was carrying something for Willow, and her side of the room filled quickly with boxes, musical instruments, painting supplies, books, and a new computer system with multiple monitors, a music keyboard, a sound-editing panel, a video-editing panel, and a digital art pad.

Willow's brother, Micah, and her parents were open and friendly. Her mother and father were students at TFSU in art and music in the 1970s and still looked the part. They had a successful art and music store in one of the fashionable rural art colonies in the state. Once everything was unloaded, Willow's family left for home. As the women chatted and unpacked they learned each other's story, and Willow understood the depth of the differences between their backgrounds and didn't comment on it. With Willow in the lead, they headed off to dinner. Willow subtly led the way, doing things first so Whitney Page could watch and learn without her lack of knowledge and skill becoming an issue. After dinner they walked through campus, again with Willow leading the way, to see where their classes might be.

Because of her scholarship Whitney Page got a new laptop from the school, but she had used computers only at school so her technology skills were limited. She had no idea how some of the software programs worked. Afraid she would hurt the laptop, she didn't try each program to explore its capabilities. Willow's workstation, with two large screens, video input, music keyboard input, and multiple multimedia programs, was like an alien spacecraft to Whitney Page.

Whitney Page's mother called every Friday evening, providing moral support and encouragement. Sensing her ongoing anxiety and depression, her mother suggested that she find a church and minister to help her through these tough times. These words of encouragement and Whitney Page's faith gave her strength to make it through the first few weeks on campus. The campus counseling center, health center, career center, and even the recreation center were not on her radar as places to get help or find friends.

At the end of the first semester Whitney Page had a long tearful talk with her mother about not wanting to return to college. Her mother knew that she did not understand what Whitney Page was going through and invited their minister over to help. Over many conversations with her minister, who was college educated and came from a family like Whitney Page's, she decided to go back to college for the rest of the year. At the end of her first year Whitney Page had joined no organizations, had taken advantage of no campus events or experiences or the career center or the counseling center or the writing center. She had visited the campus health center once. The reality was that even after a year on campus Whitney Page did not know what she needed to know or do to take advantage of the out-of-class college experience. Whitney Page had gone to class, gone to the library, gone to work, spent time with friends, and her trips off campus were to church, while Willow took full advantage of campus experiences. Whitney Page and Willow were friends and lived parallel lives. Willow moved in the art and music circles, and their class and activity schedules rarely overlapped. They had breakfast together nearly every day, and Willow kept Whitney Page talking about the things that bothered her. Willow assumed that Whitney Page knew about and would seek out campus resources if she needed them.

Going home for the summer made Whitney Page realize how much she didn't like the college experience and how much stress she felt from not fitting in. As the summer moved on she made friends at her summer job and thought seriously about not going back in the fall for her second year. Only her mother's urging and her minister's support helped Whitney Page to resolve to go back to campus. During her second year she joined a faith-based organization recommended by her minister and began to become involved on campus and to make a wider circle of friends. She continued to work, having risen to breakfast dish room supervisor, and this gave her relationships with people from dining services. She declared an accounting major, something she had known only as bookkeeping when she was in high school, and did well in her course work. She began to see the job possibilities of being an accountant, and this helped motivate her to stay in school. Even at the end of her second year Whitney Page had few friends who were not people like her, she had not been to a faculty member's home, she had not spoken to a faculty member outside class, and she did not belong to any organization other than her faith-based group.

During the summer she got a well-paid bookkeeping job at the hotel where her mother worked, and she could help with the family's expenses. Family members, close and distant, came to her for financial help because she had a well-paying job, and everyone expected her to help other family members. They asked her why she was going back to college because she already had a good job. By now Whitney Page had adjusted her income expectations from hourly wages to accountancy salaries but chose not to explain that difference to family and friends. Her answer was that she would make even more money after she graduated.

Whitney Page's junior and senior years passed without her becoming engaged in campus beyond her classes. Family still called to ask her for money and could not understand why she couldn't help during the school year. She continued to have a campus job, and all of her money went toward school basics. Because her major required it, she had visited the career center and had participated in networking and etiquette dinners. Even though she was among the top students academically in accounting, she was planning on going back home and working there. The idea of a career, of moving to a different city for work, was totally foreign to her. The idea of an extra year of study to become eligible for the certified public accountant exam was not something she ever considered.

After graduation she had a difficult job search. Her grades and recommendations were excellent, and her work as a bookkeeper during the summers demonstrated accounting experience, but she had no extracurricular experiences, no leadership training, no social capital, and no cultural capital that recommended her for work. Employers knew that any accounting major from TFSU would be able to do accounting, especially one with grades like Whitney Page's. Coplin (2003) said that employers are looking for evidence of interpersonal skills, and these are typically built during out-of-class experiences.

Whitney Page just didn't have any evidence of building new interpersonal skills, and her interpersonal skills reflected the skill set she brought to college. Because she had few interactions with people who had a prestige dialect, prestige social skills, prestige dress, and prestige manners she appeared interpersonally much the same as she did on her first day at college. In spite of being one of the top academic graduates she finally found an accounting job in a business near her home. The job paid only three quarters of what other top students made when they started; even so, she made nearly twice her mother's salary.

Her transition to life after college was difficult. She had a better income than her parents and peers, her own apartment, her own car, and money to manage. No one had ever helped Whitney Page learn about insurance, credit, leases, retirement accounts, professional liability insurance, and all the other things required for daily living after college. Family members continually asked her for money and help, so it was difficult for her to save money, and consequently she sank into credit debt.

(I am indebted to Khou Yang, Christina Armstrong, and Tradara Sprowel for their courage and honesty in sharing stories from their college experiences.)

## So what?

Whitney Page can be seen as a commuter student even though she lived in the residence halls for four years. Going to class, going to work, and hanging out with her friends from similar backgrounds were her primary college experiences. The college experiences for Willow, Michelle, Misty, and Ursula were foreign to Whitney Page. Not knowing the value of the cocurriculum (non-credit-bearing campus events like leadership workshops), the value of prestige social skills, dialect, or interpersonal skills led Whitney Page to not participate in those experiences that would have added to her skill set. It was crucial that Whitney Page spend time with people from her background, and it was equally crucial that Whitney Page spend time with people who could help her learn a new skill set without disrespecting the skill set she brought to college.

Without conscious interventions, in Whitney Page's case by her minister, many working/poverty-class students do not get to campus or persist once they are there. On TFSU campus, interventions aimed at first-generation students, toward working/poverty-class students, are available from the federally funded TRIO programs office and target students who have been identified as coming from disadvantaged backgrounds. These programs are marginalized on campus because they deal with students deemed less academically talented because they generally have lower grades and lower test scores than other students. The reality is that students in poor-quality schools get lower grades and lower test scores on average (Sacks, 2007). By marginalizing students and staff in TRIO programs, members of the majority campus social class are blaming economically disadvantaged students for their economic status. But because Whitney Page had excellent grades and test scores she was not on the list for being at risk.

## Louise's story

In high school Louise was not automatically placed in the college preparation classes. The staff in her school system assumed that after graduation Louise would go to a community college or would find work at home. Because she was rarely told that she could accomplish what she wanted and that she could be successful in school and that she had academic self-efficacy, her belief that she could succeed in school was low. She felt she needed to ask permission to do things, to take classes, to take advantage of services in school. This made her reserved in dealing with school staff, and Louise didn't take advantage of opportunities in high school.

Louise didn't have the knowledge or skill to manage the financial aid process. Fortunately, a college financial aid office held a workshop in a nearby town that Louise attended with her mother. Her parents had heard about the nursing and the teacher education program at TFSU and had urged Louise to pursue a major that would get her a good job. Like Whitney Page, Louise came from a world of jobs, not careers.

Louise applied to TFSU and was accepted. She was offered a full-tuition scholarship (after calculating the Pell Grant contributions) because of her grades and SAT scores, and she qualified for the college laptop giveaway program. This still left her needing $5,000 a year based on a national formula for parental contributions. While she qualified for loans over $5,000 each year, the staff at the financial aid workshop she attended strongly suggested getting a minimum amount in loans. Her parents agreed to sign for the subsidized loans so she could afford college, and she knew that she might have as much as $20,000 in debt after graduation. One of Louise's friends decided to sign up for $12,000 a year in loans, because her parents didn't want to contribute to her college education, because she didn't really understand how much debt this was going to mean, and because she assumed she would complete college and get a high-paying job. This friend quit college after two years, owing $24,000.

On move-in day Louise and her family arrived on campus with her one suitcase and one trunk of clothing and college gear. With the help of the hall staff Louise moved into her room, and the family left for home. In the room Louise felt alone and frightened. She had always had people around her and had always known how to do what needed to be done. She was not even sure what she is afraid of.

Louise was unpacking her clothes and bedding and setting up her side of the room when her roommate, Nicole, arrived. Nicole and her parents exploded into the room, greeting Louise and bringing in box after box of stuff. They were careful to put all of Nicole's things on her side of the room, not invading Louise's space. Louise felt plain in contrast to Nicole and her exciting parents, who were TFSU graduates and were trading stories about campus life, buildings remembered, and campus events from their time as undergraduates. When all the boxes were piled into the room Nicole's Dad suggested they all go for a bite to eat at The Lion's Gate and swept Louise along in their wake when they went for "a real college experience" according to Nicole's Mom.

When they were finally all jammed into a booth Nicole's Dad ordered different burgers for everyone. "You'll love this," he said as he ordered food for Louise. The food was good but the conversation was beyond her. Their talk about buildings, faculty, programs, sororities, and campus life was almost a foreign language. When queried about her major Louise said she was thinking about education. "Oh, that's a good major for a young woman." The conversation moved on to different topics. Louise felt like baggage.

The meal over, leave taking over, Louise and Nicole went back to their room and Nicole started to set up her side of the room with her princess motif, complete with pink sheets and a pink quilt from Marshall Fields. Nicole got a phone call from a friend and left when she was almost finished putting away her many outfits. Louise felt even more alone then and wanted to hide in her room.

Dinner was a trial in the dining hall. With no friends to lead the way Louise was lost in the process. One of the food service women at the door who noticed her discomfort told her how to slide her card in the reader and to take a tray and try everything. Louise was terrified. Not knowing if she had just paid for food or what had happened when she slid her card she managed to move forward, get a tray, and look around. Being smart helped her as she began to notice that people were wandering around, getting food from different areas of the serving line, and just leaving when they were done eating. Her tension about paying and about how to get food eased off somewhat. She made a slow circuit of the serving areas, made her selection, and sat down by herself nearly ready to cry, isolated, and shocked.

This story has two possible scenarios. Scenario 1: Louise eats alone, makes few friends over the semester, makes it through the semester with good grades, and once home in December decides to take a job in her hometown. Scenario 2: Mary sits down in the dining hall with Louise and says, "Hello, can I join you? I don't know anyone here." Mary is from a city and has good social skills, the kind that build social capital. Mary and Louise spend time sharing backgrounds and discover many things in common, and both share their feelings of isolation and loneliness. The next day Louise meets with her adviser and works out a schedule of classes for her first semester. Because she has not yet declared a major she is placed into many general education classes so she "can find something that interests her."

Mary and Louise, now dining room friends, make it through the first week, and then the first month, slowly getting to know more and more people who come from backgrounds like theirs. Louise finds a few people from rural backgrounds like hers, but she doesn't have the vocabulary to articulate the problems of class and of being a first-generation student. She just knows that her friends are people like her and that Nicole is not like her. Louise begins to build some new social skills. Having lived in a small town she never had to meet new people because there were rarely new people to meet.

Bandura (1982) wrote about the role of chance encounters in life paths. Louise's chance encounter with Mary qualifies as a significant life event. While it would have been great if Louise's RA had been able to provide support and introductions, the RA was very busy elsewhere on her floor, and Louise didn't know to go to the RA for help.

In class Louise was quiet. While most of her classes were large-class lectures, there were discussion sections for them. She did not typically participate in the discussions, but she always went to classes and discussion group meetings. She never met a faculty member outside class, never approached one after class, and did not speak to the teaching assistant who ran her discussion section. Other than occasional brief conversations with her RA, Louise had no contact with any TFSU employees other than food service workers.

As the semester progressed Louise began to feel more comfortable on campus and with her new friends, and she felt less comfortable with her roommate, Nicole. One particularly uncomfortable fall day, when the fall fashions were emerging in time with the changing leaves and Nicole was trying on her new fall wardrobe, Louise wandered down to Mary's room to ask, "Do I look like I dress like I'm from the farm?" Some of the women in the residence hall had made fashion adjustments when they got to campus, but Louise wore what she had come with. Louise found her fashion comparison group shifting. She knew she couldn't afford any of the things Nicole wore so she ignored the fashion magazines in their room. Since Louise had worked during school and over summers she knew how to budget money, how much she had left, and what she had to spend it on. Nicole seemed to have a never ending supply of money, readily replenished by Dad and Mom, to pay for pizza, parties, drinks, her sorority, new clothing, dates, and drugs.

Writing her first college paper Louise didn't quite know what to do or how to do it or whom to go to for help. But again, being smart helped, and she got a B. Nicole sent a copy to her mom and dad to look over and edit and she got a B. At finals time Nicole got a care package from home, as did many of the women on her floor. Louise realized that her mom and dad didn't even know what a care package was, or that they should send one. At the end of the semester Louise felt at home on campus, even though she felt distant from Princess Nicole. Winter break was an experience in contrast that shocked Louise. She realized how much she had changed on campus even in one semester. She tried to talk with her mother and father about nonpoint source pollution, population dynamics, and health care, and her parents wanted to talk about family members—aunts, uncles, cousins—corn and soybean prices, and high school sports.

While she was tempted to stay at home in the comfort and warmth of family and her hometown, Louise returned to campus for the spring. She discovered psychology and special education and started a double major. One evening returning from an African American History Month event that she really enjoyed she wondered, "Where are all the people like me?"

Louise got a job and began to have more money. As she got more money she began to look differently at Nicole's fashion magazines. What becomes affordable becomes attainable. Always a shrewd shopper she had been spending money on clothing that was built for durability rather than buying fashion brands. Louise learned to shop carefully in the outlet stores and began to build a wardrobe. She avoided obviously labeled fashions when she could because the labels reminded her of Princess Nicole.

During her first year Louise was not asked to attend any leadership workshops, and the only request for her participation came from a campus religious group. Louise felt she needed to ask permission to use campus services like the writing center, the tutoring center, the career center, or the counseling center. Because she had no one close to her with personal experience on campus Louise didn't know what was important on campus, and it was a long process for her to learn how to build the cultural capital on campus for herself. There were announcements for leadership workshops, student organizations, career days, etiquette dinners, and the many other campus activities that Misty and Ursula attended, but Louise didn't know their value and didn't go. Louise came to campus with such low-prestige academic cultural capital she didn't know what she needed to know. She didn't know what experiences would be valuable for her.

Her first summer at home was a trial for Louise. She found that her high school friends were still living at home, working at part-time jobs, and doing the same things they had done in high school. Louise worked long hours so she could save for college expenses, and her friends didn't seem to understand. They had enough money for their needs and kept asking her to join them when they went out to party. She found herself asking, "Where are the people like me?" Louise worked hard all summer, remembering the stimulation of campus, remembering the support of Mary and her circle of friends. She remembered the excitement of thinking about becoming a professional and using her knowledge of psychology and special education. Even though she dated a man from her hometown over the summer she broke off with him before returning to campus. She realized and could almost articulate the class differences growing between herself and her family and friends of origin.

Each semester Louise fitted into campus a little more, blending into the fashion and speech patterns, gaining rapidly in cultural capital. Though she still got sad when other students got a care package from home, she felt less anxious about it. Louise hadn't been to very many places, but she spent time on Google Earth looking at the cities people mention. She knew she could navigate around Venice to St. Mark's Square and around Brussels to the Grote Markt. Going home was more and more troublesome as she felt more at home on campus. The summer of her junior year Louise chose to work at an internship rather than go home. She told her family this was a good job and would help her with job prospects.

After graduation Louise found a teaching job that paid well, but she has trouble adjusting to living alone and being responsible for her own money. She had trouble with her lease. Not knowing to pay the rent monthly, she waited for the landlord to send her a bill. She had trouble with furnishing her apartment, buying full rooms of furniture on credit. She had trouble building social capital in her school, in part because her work didn't put her in contact with many teachers, and in part because she didn't have relationship-building skills. Her second year of teaching went much smoother as she found that she had a social class of origin similar to that of many of the other teachers.

(I am indebted to Christina Armstrong, Greg Harris, Khou Yang, and Gwen Rajski, who took their time, used their talent, and told me honest stories from their campus experiences.)

## So what?

Louise is slightly more engaged in the campus than Whitney Page, but not much. Louise does not build the social capital that comes from relationships with TFSU faculty and staff who have resources and that leads to getting invited to participate. TFSU faculty and staff have created their campus as an entrepreneurial environment. Resources and experiences are there if you seek them out. Whitney Page and Louise don't know the resources exist and don't have the skills to seek them out. Tinto (1993) wrote about the role of involvement in student retention, and the simple summary is that involved students who are engaged with faculty and staff outside class persist at higher rates than those who are not involved and engaged. Even though the faculty and staff at TFSU have aggressive programming efforts to involve and engage students like Whitney Page and Louise, the message fails to get through.

There are many types of involving campuses. The campus with resources that a student has to find, like TFSU, makes life difficult for Louise and students like her. The campus that brings resources to the students in the residence halls makes it easier for Louise to know about the counseling center, the career center, the writing center, the math center, and all the other campus resources that Nicole takes for granted. Is it Louise's fault that she lacks social skills to meet new people and make friends because of her hometown culture of origin? She doesn't know how to identify or use the resources on campus because there is no one to tell her about them. How can Louise become involved without the skills or the knowledge?

## Deficit model of class: Raising up the underclass

One common reaction majority class members have to Whitney Page or Louise is to raise her up. This is not a bad idea at the core but requires some deconstruction. If majority class members want to help Louise gain social, cultural, academic, and even economic capital, this is a good thing. If members of the majority culture want Louise to reject her own social and cultural capital along the way, this is a bad thing. If members of the majority culture think their social and cultural capital is better (hence the "up") than Louise's, then this is a bad thing.

College is stressful enough without the additional burden of being different. Being a member of an unrecognized minority and unmarked group is doubly tough. Being an ethnic gender minority in an unrecognized and unmarked group is probably quadruply tough.

There are many ways for students from the underclass to deal with the college experience. Whitney Page and Louise each adjusted in their own way. Brian is a first-generation student who has become successful on campus. His immigrant parents encouraged him to go to college and are financially and emotionally supportive. Brian chose to go to TFSU because of the opportunities there for involvement and because he could get a good education at a reasonable price. When he comes home on break his parents are interested in what he has learned and share in his enthusiasm for college and for fitting in.

During his time at TFSU Brian was active in student government, intramurals, and was vice president of his fraternity. He participated in six leadership workshops, and two of them involved being mentored over the course of a semester. He attended etiquette dinners, dress-for-success workshops, social networking workshops, and took a theater class to learn how to act. He read all the appropriate men's success magazines and the appropriate best sellers. As a senior Brian had perfect majority-class manners, dressed correctly for every majority class occasion, had flawless majority-class social networking skills, and was well liked by faculty and administrators.

As a senior Brian led workshops on dress, manners, etiquette, social skills, and now that he is over 21, he teaches about wine and appropriate drinking. Brian is the perfect evangelical class convert.

He more strictly adheres to the authorities of dress and manners and speech than either Misty or Ursula or their parents. Brian has chosen his social class role, and Eleanor is trapped in hers. If Brian had done all of this and did not have supportive parents, he would be increasingly alienated from his parents and his friends from high school because of his change in tastes, language, dress, and interests. College would have driven a wedge between him and his social class of origin. Brian helps to normalize the campus class and to marginalize those who do not participate in the speech, manners, dress, and tastes of that class.

## Summary

The college experience is a special problem for Louise and Whitney Page and for other students like them. Support from within and from without, from clergy, parents, RA staff, faculty, counseling and career centers, and all sources, is one way to help students become successful on campus. Administrators of programs for students like Whitney Page and Louise must be assertive in getting their attention and at the same time must not devalue these students' social class of origin.

## Experience

Seek out and listen to the story of someone from a minority social class on campus. Since not everyone is the same, even if you are a member of the minority social class on campus, others' experiences will be different from your own.

## Reflection questions

How similar is being a class minority to being a gender minority, and how different?

How similar is being a class minority to being an ethnic minority, and how different?

Are minority statuses, such as religion, sexual preference, national background, or others, similar to being a class minority?

## Discussion questions

Is it fair to classify people as minority?

Does labeling people as class majority and class minority lead to separation and divisiveness?

Does not recognizing class differences have a negative impact on economically, socially, and culturally disadvantaged students?

Should people like Whitney Page and Louise have special programs designed to help them with their transition to college?

What are the pressures and barriers people face as they move up in social class? What will they need to learn and acquire to move into a higher class?

Is someone who wants to move up in class and works hard at it a "class traitor" to others in their social class of origin?

Do you think students from the minority class, like Whitney Page and Louise, are more likely to quit school at your campus?

# CHAPTER 7

# The Campus Ecology of Class

As EACH PERSON has a social class, so does each campus. As there are multiple ways to explore each person's social class, there are multiple ways to explore each campus's social class. Strange and Banning (2001) wrote about the campus human aggregate, the campus physical environment, the campus organizational environment, and the constructed campus environment. The human aggregate approach to environments rests on the characteristics of the people in the environment, for example, campus characteristics such as average student SAT/ACT/GRE scores; modal students' dress, cars, and language; and average student/parent/faculty/staff disposable income. Similarly, the campus physical plant reflects the campus social class environment. The way we all attribute class to objects in the physical environment leads to the assumption that high-prestige campuses have more prestigious architectural and physical features, and the assumption that if a campus has high-prestige architecture and physical features, then it is a high-prestige campus. The campus organizational environment reflects stakeholder needs and campus values. Higher social class students will have different needs from lower social class students. Consequently, campus organizations reflect perceived student needs. The constructed social class environment, seen in the light of social class as a social construct, reflects the collective beliefs of the campus members.

## The campus social class human aggregate

Birds of a feather flock together. John Holland (1973) explained that a match between each person's interests and the interests of people in a work setting is the core of a satisfying vocational choice. Misty will be most satisfied in a work experience where she shares interests with other people at work. We are all most comfortable around people like ourselves. Misty's father got a discount at Hilton Hotels, and even though the family had enough money to stay anywhere, the family wanted the Hilton experience because the family members felt comfortable in those hotels. Like colleges, hotel chains attract a specific human aggregate, a specific market segment. Why do we see the same people at our grocery store and at the movies and theater performances we attend? During her college search Ursula will seek out a campus with a significant international human aggregate. Whitney Page and Louise may try to find a four-year campus with people like them.

*Gender and ethnicity.* A simple model of a human aggregate environment would be a classroom of entirely women. It would be even simpler if that classroom was on an all-women's campus so that the out-of-class environment mirrors the in-class environment. The human aggregate environment would be women. At the few remaining men's colleges the human aggregate would be men. At HBCUs the human aggregate would be African Americans. Each women's college, each men's college, each HBCU, each tribal college, each religious institution has a human aggregate based on gender or ethnicity or culture or religion that is part of its campus culture. If the choice is available students seek out campus environments that reflect who they are, that reflect shared values, norms, culture, gender, ethnicity, belief, or religious affiliation.

*The average.* One key feature of any human aggregate environment is the norm, the middle, the average. On most campuses Misty and Ursula are average, even though they are not average when considering the total U.S. population. Applying the principles of human aggregate as a way to examine campus social class climate yields interesting results. The two largest minority groups on most campuses are men and first-generation students. The percentage of first-generation students on a four-year campus is typically 25%, with highly selective campuses having fewer and open-access campuses having more (Ishitani, 2006). How many does it take to make a majority? In a meeting with 15 women and 5 men the women are an arithmetic majority, but which group sets the norms? Majority in numbers does not mean a cultural majority. The weight of numbers needs to be balanced against the power and prestige of the members present.

A majority of first-generation students on a campus will probably result in a small overall effect on the campus social class culture; not all members of the campus community have equal weight in creating the aggregate. Faculty and administrators have a powerful influence on campus culture. Campus has lumpy demographics with groups like the Greeks, athletes, honors students, art students, and all the other visually identifiable groups. Working/poverty/underclass students will create a group of their own, but it will not have much of an overall effect on campus because their norms, their embodied cultural capital, are devalued. On some highly selective prestige campuses the norms, values, food, music, and fashion of the lower classes are actively ridiculed.

The social class human aggregate of an environment is one way to explore the norms of the culture, food, music, and fashion. Students on any campus will flock to the familiar. Agriculture majors will hang out with other agriculture majors. Fraternity men and sorority women will hang out with each other. Students in work-study jobs will recognize each other and form a loose alliance based on social class of origin. Campuses have a lumpy human aggregate, and that is a good thing.

However, not all lumps are considered equal, and that is a bad thing. Classic college-ranking criteria, like average student SAT scores, number of high school advanced placement classes completed per student, average advanced placement test scores, number of National Merit students, and other descriptions are a human aggregate view of the campus. Students from wealthy families are far more likely to score high on each of these criteria, resulting in a high national ranking for the school.

## The campus social class physical environment

Ivy-covered buildings, tree-lined walks, the college pond, and the grassy quad are all images of the prestige campus. Boyer (1988) noted that students are attracted to water and mature trees on campus. There is meaning in space. We all have class-based stereotypes of campuses in spite of evidence to the contrary. Columbia/Barnard, Harvard/Radcliffe, and Brown/Pembroke are all in urban centers. Our images of the Ivy League and Seven Sisters come to us from Princeton, Mount Holyoke, Dartmouth, Smith, and Cornell, which have pastoral settings featuring tree-lined streets, open green spaces, mature trees, and old well-maintained buildings.

Issues of architecture aside, the tools of symbolic interaction (White, 1949) come into play in making meaning of the buildings and objects on a campus. "Riddle me this, Batman. When is a chair not a chair?" The answer is, "When it is an Eames lounge chair and ottoman." At some point a chair stops being a chair and becomes an icon and appears on a U.S. postage stamp. The chair is no longer just a chair because we each act differently toward an object based on our knowledge of that object. Knowing about an Eames chair, either the iconic teak plywood lounge chair and ottoman version or one of the fiberglass models, is social capital. It is knowledge typical of a U.S. social class, and using the precepts of symbolic interaction, the meaning is transmitted socially and modified through interpretation.

This mode of transmission of meaning is no longer wholly interpersonal. It is possible to Google "Eames lounge chair and ottoman" and learn about it, which is not a social transmission in the traditional sense, and it is possible to modify your knowledge through interpretation without ever having seen or sat in this chair. To do this you must first be told about the chair or learn about it in some way. Blumer (1969) wrote about the social transmission of knowledge before Google (BG), before Wikipedia (BW), and before YouTube (BYT), so knowledge of the chair was interpersonally and socially transmitted. The experience of an Eames chair BG, BW, and BYT was immediate and tactile. Now that experience is an Internet image, a wiki entry, and a YouTube video. That is, if you know to look, you know this is an object with valued meaning among a certain class group. The meanings of buildings, objects, and events that fill the campus is social capital, portable wealth in the form of knowledge. How much time is or was spent teaching you the meanings of buildings, objects, and events on your campus?

The physical environment social class cues on any campus come in sizes from nano to macro. The objects on the bookcases in my office represent the nano end of the size spectrum. I have a bowl of coins from my trips around the world. The classed meaning of one coin is interesting, as is the classed meaning of a bowl full of coins from 30 different nations. On the midscale of objects there are offices and buildings. Design elements in buildings provide class cues. On the macro scale is the campus. Miami University in Oxford, Ohio, has a singular architecture. Each building is made of red brick with white trim, white pillars, and a copper roof. The physical environment projects a classed message.

## The campus social class organizational environment

The organization of any campus administration reflects campus values and the perceived needs of stakeholders. If students need career guidance there will be a career center; if students need counseling there will be a counseling center. If there is a perception that students need support and help in adjusting to the campus social class environment there should be an office for that. Unfortunately, that is not often a perceived need, and underclass students don't have an advocacy group like many other minority groups that can get organizational structures put into place to help.

Human relations on campus reflect the majority social class. Faculty members and administrators vie for power primacy on campus while staff and students vie for last place. Campus organization charts never include students. Campus administrators' emphasis on leadership development rather than on membership development reinforces class structures in which some people have more than others. Campus leadership programs choose students with leadership experience gained in high school to participate in leadership experiences on campus. This limits the availability of these experiences to other students and perpetuates an ongoing class structure reinforced through formal organizations.

Alternative models of leadership and organizational structure meet with derision and disbelief. How can groups perform without traditional leadership? This question should read as, "How can groups perform without leadership as I have been led to understand it?" Any system that creates a hierarchy of power, authority, and privilege is by its very nature classed and by its very nature perpetuates class. The current administrative and leadership order gives privileges and advantages to some and disadvantages to others. The lack of wide acceptance of more inclusive models of leadership should confirm the robust nature of the classed belief in hierarchical control in organizations.

## The campus social class constructed environment

The constructed environment comes from the phenomenological tradition of examining the collected perceptions, collected beliefs, and aggregate norms in a social setting. "We're number one" is a collective belief and is part of the constructed environment. The statement is true because we believe it to be true. Changing the human aggregate environment means changing the people, and changing the constructed environment means changing the people's perception of the environment.

Moos (1974) performed a factor analysis on measures of psychological environments, and he revealed three primary social climate factors: (a) a relationship dimension, (b) a personal growth and goal orientation dimension, and (c) a system maintenance and change dimension. From these three factors Moos developed numerous assessments, including the university residence environment scale used to assess social climate in that context. The social climate is computed as the aggregate of the answers that residents have about their hall environment. The assessment relies on what people believe to be true about their environment.

Similar to Moos, but bereft of the factor analysis, is the work of Hofstede and Hofstede (2006) in developing a terminology to make distinctions between cultures. They identified five cultural dimensions: (a) power distance, (b) individualism, (c) masculinity versus femininity, (d) uncertainty avoidance, and (e) long-term versus short-term orientation. The Hofstedes based their concepts on decades of working with employees of multinational corporations. They maintained that cultures vary on these five dimensions, which are cultural norms or widely held beliefs among members of the culture.

Moos's model or the Hofstedes' model can be used to describe the constructed environment of a campus along the dimensions they describe. Using class as an overlay to either model raises questions about differences between class subcultures. How does Whitney Page's social class culture of origin construct individualism or the personal growth and goal orientation dimension, and how is that different from the constructed environment on Eleanor's social class culture of origin? These models provide a language to describe a campus and to make distinctions between campuses. As well, these provide a convenient way to contrast students' social class cultures of origin and compare and contrast them with the campus constructed environment.

Other descriptions of cultural norms also provide effective tools to examine the constructed environment of the campus. One underlying idea in the seminal work *Anti-Intellectualism in American Life* (Hofstadter, 1963) is that in the United States there is an ongoing history of anti-intellectualism and an emphasis on the practical at the expense of the theoretical or ideal. This can be applied to campus life. While a campus is supposed to represent the intellectual life and value the intellectual as a person and as a lifestyle choice, this is not always the case. Dews and Law (1995) in *This Fine Place So Far From Home* make the point that anti-intellectualism serves to perpetuate class structure. People in the poorer classes, burdened by poor-quality schools, eschew education and celebrate physical labor as real work that has moral benefits. Stereotypically, members of the underclass see nonlabor as morally deficient work for morally deficient people. The constructed social class cultural attitudes toward school help reproduce the education gap between rich and poor.

## Summary

Where you start matters. Where you start provides some interesting analytical tools. Starting with class as a campus-based phenomenon leads to campus ecology analytical tools. The human aggregate of campus, the physical reality of campus, and the organizational structures of campus are multiple ways to see class on campus. These are also multiple ways to become aware of class on campus. Using a class lens to view how we all cocreate and coevolve the ideas of class on campus is informative and highlights our role in the interpersonal processes.

## Experience

Walk around a campus, camera in hand, and take photos of buildings or locations or offices or spaces that reflect what you believe to be lower class and higher class for your campus. Create an annotated photo presentation, including your commentary on why certain things are classed the way you perceive them to be.

## Reflection questions

How is the human aggregate, the majority class culture, similar to or dissimilar to your previous experience in school or on another campus? What does this mean for your behavior every day?

## Discussion questions

Is it fair to assign class values to objects, buildings, and spaces?

Describe a stereotypical upper-class social party and a stereotypical lower-class party. What is the decor? How do the people interact? What do the people eat or drink? How do the people behave?

Describe a stereotypical upper-class faculty member's or administrator's office on your campus and a stereotypical office from a different class. What is the difference in design and decor for the president's office and the financial aid waiting room on your campus? What message does this send to students?

How do faculty administrators use their office space, furniture, and decorations to send a class message?

What are some common beliefs, the constructed environment, about people from the minority class on your campus?

# PART TWO

# *Manifestations of Social Class*

THE CHAPTERS IN PART TWO explore different models of social class in some detail. There is no single all-encompassing model of class, and multiple models are an effective way of understanding and using class on campus. As with multiple models of photons, multiple models of class are relevant and useful. As with multiple types of screwdrivers, the type you use depends on the screw you need to drive.

# CHAPTER 8

# *Class as Income and Wealth*

INCOME IS ONE SCOREKEEPER for social class that drives and reflects how concepts of class, value, and prestige change. It is temptingly simple to use an income model of class, but it neglects all manner of other important differences between people. In some ways the amount workers are paid reflects the extent to which their work is valued in the marketplace of employment. In other ways the laws of supply and demand come into play in determining salary. In still other ways wages are affected by nonmarket forces like union contracts or being in a position to move massive amounts of money into and out of a stock market. And in yet other ways employees' ability to generate income, directly or indirectly, affects salary. Baseball players generate income for their corporations. Attorneys generate income for their corporations. Farmhands picking lettuce generate income for the farmer's corporation.

## A case study

Richard and Robert grew up in the same midsize town, went to the same church, were in the same Scout troop, and played football together in high school. After high school Robert got an hourly wage job alongside his father at MidWorld Manufacturing, which had contracts with an Asian auto manufacturer and with NASA in the United States. Richard went to the regional state college where his father and mother had gone. He met and married René, and they both got a degree in business management and accounting. After college Richard got a management job at MidWorld Manufacturing, and his wife got a management job at the bank where Robert's wife was a teller. Richard's starting salary was only slightly more than Robert's. Richard and Robert both bought homes on the same street. Based on income Richard and Robert are of the same social class because they have the same income. Based on other factors, they are not. They don't socialize with each other, their wives don't participate in the same community activities, they don't vacation at the same destinations or watch the same TV programs or read the same magazines and newspapers or have the same drinking habits. They just have a similar income.

## Multiple views of class groups based on income

We can create income groups based on family income by employing the quintile groups used by the U.S. Census Bureau (2008b). Using common language for class we get the following naming scheme:

Upper-middle class—highest 20% income
Middle-middle class—second highest 20% income
Lower-middle class—middle 20% income
Working class—second lowest 20% income
Lower class—lowest 20% income

There are obvious problems with this scheme. First, there is no group named the "upper class" in this naming scheme. The upper 20% income group includes a wide range of incomes encompassing even the elite wealthy. We could subdivide the top 20% group, but this gives special favor to the elite wealthy by creating a group for that small percentage with significant wealth. Second, the middle class in this naming scheme is really the top 60%, the combination of the upper-middle, middle-middle, and lower-middle class groups. The character

Verbal Kint in *The Usual Suspects* (Singer, 1995) notes, "The greatest trick the devil ever pulled was convincing the world he didn't exist. And like that . . . he is gone." The upper 20% income controls the language of class. We, the members of that group, write the books, study about class, teach, control the media, and control education. In an unconscious conspiracy we have used the classification scheme to convince people that the upper 20% are the upper-middle class, and like that . . . we are no longer the upper class, having changed our name.

We can adjust this class-naming scheme and call the middle group the middle of the middle class:

Upper—highest 20%
Upper-middle class—second highest 20%
Middle-middle class—middle 20%
Lower-middle class—second lowest 20%
Lower class—lowest 20%

This naming scheme has the advantage that the middle 60% is the middle class, but what has happened to the working class in this scheme? What has happened to the lower/poverty class in this naming scheme? We could adjust the class names to upper, upper middle, middle, working, and poverty, and the lower-middle class disappears. We could shift to seven groups and adjust the names appropriately. The reality is that any grouping we use has some problems that challenge the usefulness of income as a simple measure of class. Next time you read about class names, pay attention to how they are being defined. We could expand the number of class groups to seven or even nine and find appropriate names for them. But if they are equally sized groups then the top group should properly be called the upper class and the bottom group should properly be called the lower class. Naming class based on income is one of many schemes for naming class.

## Income as more than income

Class as income has the advantages and disadvantages of being simple. Money in and of itself is meaningless. How people spend their money is important when understanding class. Money can buy material things and experiences. Money can buy tutoring, music lessons, trips to museums, language lessons, designer handbags, alcohol, drugs, sex, legal assistance, and a lot of other things that are part of an individual's social class. When class is seen more complexly, it is not money that determines someone's class but the experiences that money provides. People in different classes will shop at different stores, regardless of their income. If someone from the upper 20% income group shops at Walmart what does that say about his or her class standing? Is he or she to be considered among the moneyed working class? Fashion branding, positional goods, is an association between money and class. If you can purchase an obviously labeled product, then you must belong to a moneyed class. Conversely, if you purchase a down-market product, even obviously labeled, you must belong to the nonmoneyed class.

## So what?

When income is used for a central metaphor of class on campus, then the implications are economic. Tuition, room, and board costs are one way to separate the classes economically for the admissions process. Financial aid is the force that pushes against the economic separation of students, and the campus ecology of class is reflected in every campus's financial aid and tuition strategy.

Seen on an individual level, income is a significant way to separate students in a university. The costs of organizational memberships, social events, supplemental readings, technology hardware, or just socializing with friends are among the many reasons income continues to separate students into classes on every campus. Shifting the cost burden onto students is not recognized as a class issue even when it is an economic necessity. Research (e.g., Tinto, 1993) overwhelmingly indicates that involvement is one key for college success, and if involvement comes at a cash price, economically disadvantaged students will not become as involved as those with ready cash or credit.

## Class as wealth

Income is potential wealth, or net worth. Individuals can be divided into two groups: The wealthy have more than they owe, and the non-wealthy owe more than they have. As you might imagine wealth is not distributed evenly in the United States. The few people with wealth control a lot of the money in the country. Wealthy people have wealth, but if you have wealth, are you wealthy? Having $144,700 in home equity does not make you wealthy because it is different from having $144,700 in cash or something easily turned into cash. The reality is that most people don't save much money and don't accumulate much wealth. People who do accumulate wealth typically don't accumulate large amounts of wealth. The reality is that most personal wealth is under the control of a very small number of people.

*Us and them: The middle income class and the other income classes.* A simple wealth-based view of class yields the poor, the middle class, and the wealthy. If I can see myself as middle class, then I am like other people. The poor and the wealthy get the media attention, and the middle class gets remembered during political campaigns. The middle class gets stretched during election year to include Joe the Plumber, who had a $250,000 income. In the media the middle class has become bigger, ever more inclusive, and ever more normal. The *other* people, the poor and the wealthy, are not normal; they are not people like us. *We* are the normal *us,* and *they* are the abnormal deviant *others.* Some campaign speeches emphasize the pride of the working man and woman, the subtext in that speech being that working men and women are nearly normal, are nearly *us.* The meaning is that it is nearly normal to be working class and almost people like us, not one of the others. The others are the wealthy and the poor. An implication here is that the working poor should want to be like people like us.

Wealth is a good marker for students from higher-class families. The median family income in 2007 for families whose head of the household was between 45 and 54, and probably with college-age children, was $182,500 (U.S. Census Bureau, 2009). This money reflects mostly home equity and not assets like cash, stocks, or bonds. That amount,

$182,000, is about enough cash to send two children to a public university for four years as in-state students, or one child to a private college or an out-of-state public university for four years. The interest income generated from this wealth is enough for community college tuition for one child who still lives at home.

*The media fiction wealthy.* Wealthy people are certainly entertaining. There is a small number of media celebrities and a smaller number of wealthy celebrities, yet these few people occupy a disproportionate amount of media space. Our fascination with the wealthy who have celebrity status has served as a way to entertain people, sell newspapers, books, and media for centuries. One consequence of this focus on wealth is that the upper class becomes a media fiction. "Let me tell you about the very rich. They are different from you and me." (Fitzgerald, 2005). This media attention given to very wealthy people, who are a small minority in the United States, reinforces the view of an upper class that does not include those in the upper 20% for U.S. household income. The myth is that the upper class is the very wealthy, while the reality is that the upper class in the United States is those in the upper 20% of household income, even though we self-identify as upper-middle class.

## So what?

The implications for wealth on campus are the same as for income. The potential to donate money for a building should not be an admissions criterion, yet it has been used that way. Wealth brings with it connections, or social capital. The sons and daughters of the bankers and lawyers and business executives may not be clever or even academically talented, but the sons and daughters of these bankers, lawyers, and business executives get preferential handling in admissions. Using money as a way to assign people to classes has the advantage of being easy. It has the disadvantage of limiting the discussion of class to the discussion of money. It has the disadvantage of being imprecise so that the idea of the middle class can extend well into the upper, upper income levels. All in all, money is an easy but severely limited view of class. Social class is more than money.

## Experience

Find out or estimate, based on research, your family income for last year, and determine where you stand in comparison to other people in the United States.

Learn the average starting salary for someone in your chosen field working in a city near you.

Learn the average cost of living (housing, food, insurance, etc.) in a city near you.

Learn some basic information about the demographics of class, income, educational attainment, access to campus, graduation, and student success, especially on your campus.

What is the number of first-generation students on your campus?

How many Pell Grant students are on your campus?

How many legacy students are on your campus?

What is the average debt load of college graduates on your campus?

What are the graduation rates on your campus by income group?

How many faculty or administrators on your campus were themselves first generation or second generation or third generation?

Which are the majors that get the most first-generation students?

Which majors attract the most second- and third-generation students?

## Reflection question

How does knowing your income, or what your income will be after you graduate, change or confirm what you believe about social class and money?

## Discussion questions

In what way is money a good measure and in what way is money a poor measure of social class?

What are the different types of people's attitudes toward talking about money and income?

Which groups have difficulty talking about money, and which find it easy, and why do you think this is true?

Is money the most common way you assign people to social class? If not, how do you assign people to classes?

How do you know how much money someone has without asking him or her?

How do you let other people know how much money you have?

Do you ever lie about how much money you have or don't have?

How important is money to you?

# CHAPTER 9

# Class as Capital

KARL MARX (1885) championed the idea that class was about capital and control over the means of production. Control over production creates capital for those in control. To Marx capital was money, capital was solely economic. While that analysis worked well at one point in history, the limitations of money as the marker for class are clear, and the number of people who control large amounts of personal capital in the manufacturing sector is small. Most capital is now controlled by corporate executives and corporate boards.

## Bourdieu on capital

Pierre Bourdieu (1986), a French Marxist sociologist, suggested in *The Forms of Capital* that capital should be seen more broadly and include economic, cultural, and social capital. This expanded idea of capital serves as a much better tool for understanding class than using only income or wealth. Economic capital was covered in the previous chapter, so this chapter starts with cultural capital. Bourdieu described three forms of cultural capital: embodied, objectified, and institutionalized.

*Embodied cultural capital.* This kind of capital is immaterial, it is personal knowledge and skill, and it takes time and effort to accumulate embodied cultural capital. Embodied capital cannot be inherited;

it must be accumulated firsthand with hard work and homework. Formal and informal education produce this form of cultural capital. Of course it is easier to accumulate embodied cultural capital at home at an early age if you live a wealthy life rather than a poor life. Experiences build cultural capital, but not all of them take money. Museums, art galleries, national parks, state capitols, and many other venues that build cultural capital are low cost. "The social conditions of its transmission and acquisition are more disguised than those of economic capital, it is predisposed to function as symbolic capital, i.e., to be unrecognized as capital and recognized as legitimate competence" (Bourdieu, 1986, p. 245). It is hard to accumulate cultural capital on campus if you don't come to campus with some measure of experience. It would be like learning baseball by starting in the Major Leagues trying to hit balls thrown by a serious pitcher who doesn't want you to hit the ball. Then if you do get a hit you need to move forward a base at a time by relying on others to hit a fast, spinning, and often curving round ball with a round bat. Barry Switzer, quoted in chapter 3, would agree: Being born on third base is a much easier way to make a run.

Someone who is cultured possesses embodied cultural capital. One purpose of general education on campus is to have students accumulate embodied cultural capital by studying science, humanities, math, literature, art, theories, research, and people. The faculty gets to decide what is taught, and this further reinforces the idea that faculty members are gatekeepers for the upper classes. Our advanced degrees are evidence of embodied cultural capital in our discipline. Attaining a PhD or terminal degree is a socialization process. Faculty members have a general agreement that what they read in college is what you should read in college. This makes sense from the point of view that faculty members are the conservators of our cultural heritage. The overlay of gender and ethnicity on what gets read in general education classes is a topic deserving of a long conversation. The overlay of class on what gets read in these classes sits in the corner waiting to be invited into the conversation.

One limitation of Bourdieu's idea is that embodied cultural capital is not homogeneous across all class cultures and subcultures. The idea of prestige cultural capital needs to overlay Bourdieu's idea of embodied cultural capital, creating the idea of prestige embodied cultural capital. Three modifiers for capital are cumbersome but this distinction between prestige and nonprestige embodied cultural capital is important. Faculty members place value on prestige embodied cultural capital, as they define it, and typically devalue nonprestige embodied cultural capital, as they define it. Poetry classes are far more likely to include e. e. cummings than cowboy poetry. Knowing the standings of NASCAR drivers does not have the cachet on campus as knowing the difference between a Pinotage and a Pinot Noir. Our educational institutions, especially selective liberal arts colleges, transmit embodied prestige cultural capital.

First-generation college students come to campus with limited prestige embodied cultural capital. They may know NASCAR, but they have limited knowledge and skills of the prestige forms of address, fashion sense, dialect and variety of speech and accents, table manners, interpersonal rituals, food preferences, music, art, theater, film, and the numerous components of the prestige class. Further, the nonprestige embodied cultural capital, the cultural knowledge and skills of these first-generation students, is not valued by faculty members and is even ridiculed by faculty and students at selective campuses.

The transmission of prestige embodied cultural capital is disguised. Jack and Jill clubs, Junior League, and other institutions like these serve as vehicles for the transmission of capital as much as Future Farmers of America and 4-H. It is just a different set of knowledge and skills that each of these organizations transmits, and all of these organizations reproduce the social class structure by passing on embodied cultural capital. The role of the university in transmitting prestige embodied cultural capital is widely recognized and rarely discussed. The role of the university in selecting the students who have a lot of prestige embodied cultural capital is celebrated in collegiate rankings.

*Objectified cultural capital.* This is stuff, material objects, that can be touched, bought, and sold. You can easily transform economic capital into objectified cultural capital: You can purchase a painting. The problem of prestige and objects raises some issues. A painting of Elvis on velvet is not as prestigious as a painting of a dancer by Degas. Owning an object and appreciating an object are quite different. Owning a computer and being able to use its features are quite different.

Prestige objectified cultural capital gets an interesting translation when applied to U.S. education and the consumer society. When a college education is seen as a commodity, as a consumer product like a painting, we can identify luxury educations, mass-market educations, and discount educations. Objectified cultural capital can be purchased, but embodied cultural capital takes time and effort to accumulate. You cannot purchase an education like you purchase a painting.

*Institutionalized cultural capital.* Certificates of cultural competence, like diplomas, are the currency of institutionalized cultural capital. U.S. businessmen and businesswomen display their first dollar, and academics display their diplomas, evidence of institutionalized cultural capital, as evidence of success. As with other forms of cultural capital, the prestige factor is important here also. A diploma from Indiana State University does not have the same prestige as a diploma from Indiana University or a diploma from Stanford University. U.S. accrediting agencies have standardized a college degree based on credit hours, which typically translates into seat time. While credit hours are supposed to be exchanged on par between universities, credit hours from a lower-prestige university are often not acceptable at a higher-prestige university. Flimsy reasons bereft of evidence are used for this practice. "Their classes are not as good as ours. Their faculty are not as good as ours. So we won't transfer their credits for our degree."

## Bourdieu on social capital

The single best phrase about social capital came to me from Michael Cuyjet: "It's not who you know, it's who knows you." In days gone by social capital was the old boys' network, and in the contemporary world it is your social network. The role of social networking software in building and maintaining social capital, loose ties and strong ties, is growing, and some writers have examined the class implications of different social networking sites (boyd, 2007). Building social capital, like building embodied capital, takes time and skill. Propinquity certainly makes building social capital easier. Going to the right country clubs, the right social events, and the right prep schools and colleges aids in being near people with resources. Even at college, belonging to the right club, organization, or political group helps by being near others who may become part of a social network.

As with other forms of capital there is prestige social capital and nonprestige social capital. It is certainly more prestigious social capital for faculty members on campus to include deans and vice presidents in their social network than to include junior faculty. No wonder junior faculty feel left out. Similarly, it is advantageous (social capital) for students to include faculty in their social network and certainly more advantageous than creating a social network of drinking associates. The value of social capital is the level of resources available to the social network.

## Other kinds of capital

*Academic capital.* Academic capital is currency on a campus and should have its own category because of its importance. The ability to read well, take notes well, write well, participate in class discussions well is the skill set of academic capital. The knowledge base for academic capital, akin to embodied cultural capital, reflects all the prestige knowledge that students are supposed to have. When a professor talks about the Arc de Triomphe, Sugarloaf Mountain, *Mending Wall*, or carte blanche, the student is supposed to know what these are, regardless of the fact that the professor learned it after college to fit in with academic colleagues and has never been to Paris or Rio de Janeiro nor heard Robert Frost reading his poem.

If college is to help students build capital, then first-year experiences should include learning experiences on academic capital skills and academic knowledge that are the core of their curriculum. While many campuses have first-year-experience classes, they rarely have a curriculum based on enhancing student academic or cultural or social capital, or on teaching the skills that students need to build these forms of capital. Even students like Misty, Ursula, and Eleanor can stand to increase their academic capital wealth.

*Leadership capital.* Leadership capital is currency in the classroom and in the cocurriculum. The ability to work successfully with students and staff, to provide leadership, and to be a good member is an essential college and workplace skill set and knowledge base. Students who come to campus with leadership capital quickly take on leadership positions and build more capital. The rich get richer. Students who come to campus without leadership capital are excluded from this leadership track and are generally not invited to leadership development programs, many of which are reserved for the already leadership wealthy. The poor get poorer. If college is to help students build leadership capital, then affirmative efforts need to be made to include everyone in leardership education programs, not just the already leadership enabled who came to campus with leadership experience from high school.

*Spiritual, moral, values, and ethical capital.* These are important to many people on every campus. Wide and deep knowledge about spirituality, morality, values, and ethics is one foundaton of an educated person. Accumulating this form of capital may be a primary mission of some campuses, and even on state universities these are important topics and forms of capital.

*Language capital.* The prestige variety of English is taught on campus. Even though 30 states, as of this writing, have English as their official language, there is no official English. The prestige variety of English can be learned and become part of anyone's accumulated capital to be used in assignments and speaking. Students without languge capital are at risk in academic assignments, in-class discussions, and conversations with faculty members. This book would be read differently if it were written in a low-prestige variety of English with a dearth of obscure words and employing only Hemingwayesque simple sentence constructions.

Actor/writer/director Sylvester Stallone is considered a dolt by many language purists because his public and film utterances reflect and celebrate lower-class varieties of English. It is a flip dismissal of his ability to judge Stallone on his language. I have never met him, so I don't know anything about his personal language use. I do know that he is smart enough to write, direct, and act in movies that resonate with many people around the world. Looking at Stallone's movies using a classed lens is an interesting experience. The movie *Oscar* (Landis, 1991), featuring Stallone, is a fine broadside in the ongoing class warfare, and the upper class loses.

Code switching is the ability to use more than one language or variety of a language. Someone who is bilingual can switch between his languages easily. Someone who is bidialectal in English, who is fluent in two varieties of English, can switch between her varieties of English easily. Learning the prestige variety of English is for some students like learning a second language, and hopefully the first language, the first variety of English, is not being lost in this process. Code switching is a valuable skill for students who do not come to campus with the prestige variety of English. Balancing respecting students' dialect of origin with teaching them the prestige variety of English is an obligation of education.

## So what? Implications for campus

Obviously the work of a university or college campus is to help students increase their embodied capital. This embodied capital reflects what the prestige dominant majority U.S. culture values. The primary actors are the faculty members who each teach a tiny slice of the college education experience. Students use a baseball season metaphor for the college experience. Each class is one game in the season, and each game is slightly related to other games because you may have learned something playing the Yankees that you need when you play the Dodgers. Win enough games and you get a degree. For students using this metaphor the accumulation of capital doesn't count on the scoreboard and isn't on the test. The accumulation of capital does count in the job search process. The one with the most capital wins the best job.

A review of the curriculum (classes required for a degree) and cocurriculum (membership in organizations, leadership workshops, and all the other planned campus events) using intellectual and academic capital as a lens would prove fruitful. Not only would campus leaders be able to articulate what kinds of capital they value, they would be able to see who participates in experiences designed to build capital. The liberal arts/general education model of education, with value placed on breadth of learning in addition to a major, and the vocational model of education, with value placed on the major at the expense of general education and other forms of cultural capital, both reflect the idea that a college education is for increasing students' embodied capital. This holds whether you believe that education is for the social good or for individual benefit. The difference between a liberal arts view and a vocational view of education is what counts as capital and how it is translated into economic capital. In the liberal arts/general education view, clearly perceived as more prestigious by "real academics" than the vocational view, the type of embodied cultural capital reflects a very classed worldview, valuing critical thinking, knowledge or arts, literature, skill at communication, interpersonal relations, and other skill sets and knowledge reflected in general education and the cocurriculum. In the vocational view, the type of embodied capital is concentrated on knowledge and skills with short-term economic value—being employable at a specific job for a specific skill set and knowledge base. The difference between these worldviews of education is the value of cultural capital as it is transformed directly or indirectly into economic capital. Those in liberal arts/general education value long-term cultural capital for lifelong learning, while those in vocational education value short-term knowledge and skills for immediate employment.

## Summary

Each social class group uses different social class markers. Members of the class of educated professionals value professional knowledge and skills, and they value prestige cultural capital in all forms, from prestige diplomas to prestige consumer goods to prestige knowledge and culture. Members of the elite wealthy place a high value on social capital, on whom you know and who knows you and to whom you are related.

Different forms of capital are tools to broadly and deeply describe what can be accumulated as the result of the college experience.

## Experience

Compared to other students or to other people you know, how would you judge:
Your vocabulary and speaking skills?
Your knowledge of fine food?
Your knowledge of wine?
Your knowledge of literature?
Your knowledge of European geography?
Your knowledge of current world events?

## Reflection questions

Which do you value more: economic capital, cultural capital, or social capital? Which is more highly valued by your peers? Which will get you the best job or the quickest advancement?

## Discussion questions

Are the three forms of capital an effective way to talk about class? What do they miss?
What other forms of capital do you value, like spiritual capital or leadership capital?
Is it fair that on-campus faculty value upper-middle class/upper-class cultural capital that takes money and time to accumulate?
How many of your faculty do you think have been to Europe or anywhere else outside the United States? Where do you think they went?

Is it possible to use the Internet to accumulate cultural capital?

How many experiences, like leadership workshops or museum visits, are available this semester?

How many experiences, like leadership workshops or museum visits, have you participated in? Why have you done this?

# CHAPTER 10

# *Class as Education*

EDUCATIONAL ATTAINMENT is one classic way to describe class. The Madame Alexander doll in the graduation cap and gown is still a Madame Alexander doll. Hollingshead (1957, 1975) used educational attainment as one of his factors of social position and status. The *New York Times* (2005) included education, occupation, and income as three factors that determine class. A moment's reflection reveals that income, wealth, capital, and education overlap, each being a specific part of class. Educational attainment, getting a degree, is a certification of being around experiences that can lead to accumulated capital but is no guarantee that a student accumulated any knowledge or skill. "You can send me to college but you can't make me think!"

## Social class and the campus

Your level of education attainment and the prestige of your educational institution are both important. An associate's degree is more prestigious than a high school diploma, and a bachelor's degree is more prestigious than an associate's degree, and so on. Institutions that only grant associates' degrees are less prestigious than those that only grant bachelor's degrees and so on. Prestige, and therefore class, among colleges that grant graduate degrees increase at each level, up to the

149

research universities, which are the apex of the prestige triangle. Those prestige research universities have become prestigious because their faculty emphasize research over teaching, and research leads to notoriety, recognition, and publicity. Relying on the presence of prestige research scholars who only teach graduate students is a very questionable criterion when selecting a college for a child.

Rankings in education are largely a matter of prestige, resources, selectivity, and the wealth of incoming students (Carey, 2006). College rankings from *Playboy*, *High Times*, and *U.S.News & World Report* are based on questionable criteria, and the data collection leaves a lot to be desired in the way of scholarly rigor. These popular magazine rankings have nothing to do with students' educational experiences and learning outcomes. At least in *Colleges That Change Lives*, Pope (2000) looks at student experiences and educational outcomes; however, only a fraction of U.S. four-year colleges was examined. Carey (2006) examined colleges in Florida, mostly because of the excellent data set maintained in that state, and found that the best colleges were not the most prestigious. The editors at *U.S.News & World Report* look at expected graduation rate as compared to attained graduation rate. One would expect all of Harvard's students to graduate, but in reality only 87% of them graduate within four years, and only 98% graduate within six years.

The National Study of Student Engagement (NSSE, 2000) was developed to provide students and parents selecting colleges with more information about the college experience. A second purpose was to inform campus administrators about what their students thought of their college experience. The NSSE measures five dimensions of student engagement: (a) student-faculty interaction, (b) supportive campus environment, (c) active and collaborative learning, (d) level of academic challenge, and (e) enriching educational experiences. In their initial multicampus study NSSE researchers identified four colleges that scored in the top 20% in all five categories that year: Beloit College, Elon College, Centre College, and Sweet Briar College. The report notes: "Of course, there surely are other engaging colleges and universities among the 1,700-plus four-year colleges and universities that have not yet administered the NSSE survey" (p. 23). These four schools are well known among the college cognoscenti and are not well known among those who pay attention to popular magazine rankings.

The business of college, in light of understanding class as capital, is to increase the knowledge, skills, and embodied cultural capital of the student for short- or long-term transformation into economic capital. Students are given opportunities in classes and on campus to learn enough to find a job that pays. Any employer knows that students with a four-year degree in accounting have a basic level of accounting knowledge and skill. What employers believe—that all colleges are more or less equal in terms of learning outcomes—is justified by the research on between-college differences in learning outcomes by Pascarella & Terenzini (2005). Their research does not lend support to the popular notion that highly selective colleges provide students with learning experiences that lead to higher learning outcomes. Most employers know that what distinguishes between job applicants is their accomplishments in the cocurriculum, in the soft skills, in cultural capital, and in the social skills needed to build social capital.

Another business of college, especially among prestige highly selective colleges, is to increase students' prestige social capital that can then be transformed into economic and cultural capital after graduation. Each college graduate has social capital on graduation, and going to college with the children of the educated, the children of the successful, and the children of the wealthy certainly gives advantages to some students.

## The individual effects of education

The perceived prestige of the campus, the nature of the students who go there, and the faculty who teach there have an effect on the individual student. College characteristics are not to be underestimated when seen through a class lens. Pascarella and Terenzini (1991, 2005) as well as Feldman and Newcomb (1969) reviewed all available research on the effect of college on students. The research reviewed was mostly about individual change and development during the college years. The conclusion was that college has a long-term effect on students in every area studied. College is worth the time and effort and cost. The economic return on the investment in college is well documented, and class is more than money.

*Education and manners.* Class can be seen as a culture, and much of culture is nonverbal. The misfit between the student and the majority social class on campus is well documented and long term (Dews & Law, 1995; hooks, 2000; Nelson, Englar-Carlson, Tierney, & Hau, 2006). If we are to believe Bourdieu (1986), the transmission of the values and rituals of the prestige culture is disguised. For students who grew up in a prestige higher-class world, who have college-educated parents, parents with graduate degrees, the values, rituals, and manners of the educated class are a native language. The etiquette of the formal dinner, the forms of politeness in all their subtlety, the symbolic interactions (White, 1949), and identification of prestige objects are authentic only to those in the educated social class of origin. Building the cultural capital to identify an Eames chair and other prestige objects found in the homes of the educated class begins at home at an early age for the few coming from homes, or visiting homes, that have those objects. The disguised manner of this learning is the daily life of young people among prestige objects, manners, values, rituals, and norms.

The transmission of manners and forms of politeness on campus should be examined on a campus-by-campus basis. Certainly faculty members have some responsibility and authority for in-class behaviors. The ongoing dialogue on civility on campus is evidence of clashes over what is polite. While this discussion is often about behavior and conflict, manners (value-laden behaviors) are being taught. Behaviors in class will be translated into behaviors in staff meetings.

*Education and language.* The prestige variety of English is currency on campus. If students choose their parents wisely, based on parental use of the prestige variety of English, it will make it easier for them to succeed on campus. Whitney Page's and Louise's home variety of English is different from Misty's, Ursula's, and Eleanor's. All varieties of English are equally expressive, equally complex, and, like the animals in Orwell's (1949) *1984*, equal. It is just that one variety of English is more equal than others on campus. The transmission of the spoken and written prestige variety of English is often done in a way that devalues minority class and minority ethnicity students. The simple phrase "Use proper English" can be deconstructed to mean that whoever said it believes that whatever perceived error of enunciation or grammar was made, whatever was uttered, was improper, wrong, deficient, and low class. Most people hearing "Use proper English" take it personally, and take it as a reflection on their social class of origin, their family, their school, and their native variety of English. Many administrators, faculty, and students don't understand that there is no proper English, no academy that certifies participles and predicates, no group that declares some English proper and some English improper. There is the prestige variety of English, and this is based on what a large number of people agree is the prestige variety of English, and that changes from year to year.

For students who come to campus using a nonprestige variety of English, learning to use the prestige variety should be seen as the acquisition of a second language that goes with a second social class identity. Learning a second language does not mean losing the first language nor should it. English as a Second Language learners should not lose their Spanish, Mandarin, or Akan any more than they should lose their Costa Rican, Han, or Akan identities. However, the value structure on campus around language actively devalues all but the prestige variety, and the message that students get is that they should not use their native variety at all.

*Standing between students and faculty.* Through their work with student organizations, workshops, residence halls, and all the cocurricular activities, student affairs professionals have more contact with students than do faculty. Those professionals, especially those on the front line working directly with students, are the men and women who staff the campus residence halls, who are fresh from graduate educations, who have a different kind of contact with students than faculty members. While faculty members see students' written work on papers, student affairs professionals hear students voices in a native environment. Even though many faculty members were themselves first-generation students and had to learn the secret handshakes, values, language variety, and fashion of campus, many faculty do a poor job of passing along those lessons to other first-generation students. Many residence hall professionals never learned the roles and rituals of other classes and are consequently ill equipped to pass them on even though they have constant contact with students.

## Summary

Educational attainment is a good marker for social class, and like other markers it has limitations. A college degree is no guarantee that a student has accumulated prestige cultural capital, has social skills, or anything other than having passed 120 credit hours of classes. The educational experience requires effort and learning in more than classes if a student wants to build capital. College structures are set up to give an advantage to those who already know what resources are available and know how to get them, so students like Whitney Page and Louise come to campus at a disadvantage. Education is the key to social mobility for some and at the same time creates class segmentation.

## Experience

Make a list of how you have changed and how you will continue to change because of your education. Will you read different books, eat different foods, have a different vocabulary, wear different clothing, have different interests or different recreational activities, and so on?

## Reflection questions

What do you value in education? The money and the job it will get you? How it will change your life? The education you will get?

## Discussion questions

Is education a good investment for you? What will you get out of the time and money spent on your education? What have you gotten out of your education so far?

Who do your faculty members believe is responsible for your learning?

How do you wish the educational system had prepared you to deal with people from different classes?

How do you think the university curriculum reflects a classed set of values?

What do the university faculty and staff do that makes college part of the way social class is reproduced?

How do you feel about the prestige a degree from your college will give you?

# CHAPTER 11

## Class as Prestige

PEOPLE TALK AS IF CLASS were about money. People act as if class were about prestige.

The concept of prestige appears a lot in this book: prestige college, prestige student, prestige variety of English, class as a collection of subcultures arranged in a hierarchy of prestige, prestige capital, and even prestige obviously labeled fashions. Prestigious is what a large number of people believe to be prestigious. Behind gender and ethnicity there is a physical reality, however meaningful or meaningless. Behind class, especially when class is seen as prestige, there is no physical reality, only what a large number of people believe, that is, only a constructed psychological reality.

### A prestige experience

Try this experiment to explore the degree to which you have internalized messages about prestige and class. Following are some consumer products and experiences. What social class do you associate with each? Just use lower, middle, and higher.

Let's try some drugs. What social class do you associate with

crack
cocaine

marijuana
alcohol
Xanax

How about brands of clothing? What class do you associate with

Nike
Prada
Armani
Red Wing
Lands' End

What about fabrics? What social class do you associate with

flannel
polyester
silk
wool

What about retail stores?

Walmart
Eddie Bauer
Neiman Marcus

Car brands?

Volvo
Ford
Cadillac
ten-year-old Cadillac

Vacation destinations?

at home
at relatives' house

Florida
Hawaii
Europe

What about social class and media?

Discovery Channel
*The Bob&Tom Show*
National Public Radio
country and western music
rap and hip-hop
opera

What about sports?

NASCAR
polo
football
golf
Putt-Putt Golf

What about dialects?

"I got no dog in that fight."
"Don't mean nothing."
"Eschew obfuscation."

Places to stay?

Motel 6
Holiday Inn
Hilton Hotel

Conducting this experiment in a large room with lots of people is entertaining and educational. Participants hold up blue cards for the higher-class items (blue blood), white for the middle-class items (white collar), and red cards (debt) for the lower-class items. The degree of agreement and participants' desires to put most things into the middle class is remarkable. While the items on this list were chosen because they are obviously prestige ranked and thus classed, a moment's thought illustrates that nearly every consumer item, vacation destination, restaurant, food, or even beverage is arranged in a hierarchy of prestige; they are classed.

If you want to know your prestige-based class status you should look at the advertisements on the television channels you watch and in the magazines you read, and think about the prestige of the material being advertised. Are you getting Chevrolet and Ford advertisements or are you getting Mercedes and Saab advertisements?

## Cost and prestige

People argue that quality goods cost more than value-priced goods, and this is mostly true. The price of any object reflects manufacturing, advertising, distribution costs, and retailer profit. The cost of manufacturing a high-quality item will be more than for a low-quality item because of the increased costs of materials and workmanship. The cost of advertising an item depends on the advertising outlet. Advertising in *Architectural Digest* will have a different cost than advertising in *Popular Mechanics*. The target audience for each magazine is different and is reflected in advertising costs. Distribution costs, getting the products to you or to a store, are the same for all products, but prestige store space and well-groomed and well-spoken staff can be quite expensive. Retailer profit will be higher for a Rolex than for a Timex because of the markup, typically 100%, for each of these products. Costlier items are not necessarily higher quailty, but they are nearly always higher prestige.

One of the most interesting dynamics of class is the increasing global use of the same set of prestige expensive consumer goods as class markers. Designer labels have become a surrogate indicator of income. Obviously labeled fashions are easier to spot than the subtle cues contained in product quality, social capital, cultural capital, dialect, and other class markers. The expanding lines of designer products and the ubiquitous obviously labeled fashions are indicators of this trend. The ongoing internationalization of prestige obviously labeled fashions would suggest that prestige is becoming an important marker of class.

## Ranking and prestige

Rankings and ratings exist for colleges, cars, restaurants, movies, and hotels. Whoever publishes the rankings and ratings gets to create their criteria. "It's good to be the king." Some of the rankings and ratings have clear easy to access criteria, but few have any information on why each criterion is important. Some of the rankings have no criteria. I always look for the quote that says, "This is a good product because . . . and this is a key indicator of quality because . . ." and I never seem to find many of those. My favorite example of criteria for quality is the "Will It Blend?" videos for the Total Blender ad campaign from Blendtec (http://www.willitblend.com/). If it will blend an iPad, it will blend a milkshake.

Restaurant ratings are a good example of criteria. The *Michelin Guide* rates restaurants in five areas:

1. The quality of the products.
2. The mastery of flavor and cooking.
3. The personality of the cuisine.
4. The value for the money.
5. The consistency between visits.

At first glance this sounds good; however, who determines the mastery of flavor and cooking, and how is that scored? Is a panel of judges used? If so, what training do the judges have? No matter the answer, I don't have the cultural capital, knowledge, and skill to determine the mastery of flavor and cooking. I know something about food, flavor, and cooking but have not been trained to make these fine distinctions. I know a badly flavored and prepared bruschetta when I taste it because I have made a few, and I can tell you what is wrong only in basic terms.

When I want to know something about a restaurant, I can open a *Michelin Guide* and count the stars. I don't need to spend time accumulating the knowledge and skills to accurately rate mastery of flavor and cooking. Ratings and rankings make my life easier if I don't have the knowledge and skills to make decisions for myself. I do have the knowledge and skills necessary to rate and rank colleges, and I can make my criteria explicit in a way that relies on published data and qualitative information garnered from college community members. Are my criteria the right ones for you? Maybe, and maybe not. Are the criteria in *Colleges That Change Lives* (Pope, 2000), in *Schools That Rock* (Eliscu, 2005), in *Playboy*'s top party schools, or in the *High Times Guide to Higher Education* the right ones for you? Maybe, and maybe not. It is simpler and easier to use prestige, ratings, and rankings as a way to judge a product, a restaurant, and even college quality than it is to acquire the knowledge and skills necessary to make your own determination.

College rankings are typically prestige rankings. If they are made with good data and clear criteria they are helpful. If they are made with questionable data and unclear unpublished criteria they are useless. The *Michelin* restaurant guide criteria were easy to find. Next time you run across an article ranking colleges take a close look at the criteria and the source of the data. Be suspicious, be very suspicious, of any ranking system.

## Keeping up with the others

Obviously labeled fashions are nearly ubiquitous, even in the People's Republic of China, and they make an easily identifiable class cue. They are the modern class markers that are easy to learn. They are a contemporary ranking system with questionable criteria. It is much easier to learn a designer name and label than to learn about material quality, construction, thread count, stitch count, wool weight, rub, and other markers of clothing quality. It makes perfect sense that fashion labels have become so popular. Markers of clothing quality are the kinds of things young people learn at home and not the kinds of things that are the subject of on-campus learning experiences except in fashion-related majors.

The lust for labels is not quite ubiquitous. In India saris do not have labels. So how do Indian women know how to rank the sari on a quality and prestige scale? Fabric, decoration, and who made it are key elements to determine sari quality. Ask an Indian woman about sari quality and prepare for a very interesting lecture and perhaps even some show-and-tell as she brings sari material the next day to show you. An Indian woman's knowledge about saris is cultural capital learned at home.

## Prestige and class

What is prestige in my class may not be prestige in your class. Coach bags may be the ultimate in fashion for you and may not even make my list. A Dodge dually, twin rear wheels on each side, may be the acme of prestige for you and may be authentic to your social class of origin. A Dodge dually may be a marker for me to identify you as a prestige member of a different social class, as upper-working class. There are between-class markers, labels that cross classes, and within-class markers, labels that are unique to a social class. These markers of class change from season to season based on the vagaries of manufacturers, fame, and which celebrity is wearing what.

The sources of prestige are simple and complex. The simple answer is that marketing from direct advertising to product placement to buzz is the source of prestige. "What is today's media celebrity, singer, or football/basketball/baseball player wearing?" Product placement is an industry. Who is wearing which designer's clothing seems to occupy as many column inches as news of conquest, war, famine, and death. Unless it is a celebrity death involving drugs. The complex answer is that there is a dialogue between the people and the media.

## Prestige and college

The back of a car is a prestige billboard; the college stickers on the back window of moms' and dads' cars are signs about social class and values.

The competition among students and parents to get into a prestigious college is a fact of life for many in the middle and upper classes. As with fashion labels, college prestige has an easy answer that is widely used—college rankings. It is easier to look at some college-ranking scheme and note that your child's campus is among the best in some way than it is to take the time to become more informed about college choice based on learning outcomes, college experiences, and the many other factors that should go into the college choice process. I don't think that choosing a college should be like choosing a restaurant, but decrying college rankings is like decrying designer labels. The massive flood of media about obviously labeled products and obviously labeled colleges is too great to resist. Building the cultural capital to choose quality products is tough, whether it is a suit or a college. Simple answers based on name recognition from rankings is a real starting point for many college shoppers. It is irrelevant if the first question about a college should be, "What is your college's ranking?" Rankings are the cultural capital people use to make decisions about college. Obviously labeled colleges have become the same as obviously labeled fashion.

## Competition

Prestige is inherently a competitive interpersonal sport. You win if you have higher prestige, you lose if you have lower prestige. This competition is driven by people and enhanced by market forces. No one needs a designer handbag, but many people need a handbag. Filling a need and buying a designer obviously labeled fashion accessory are two entirely different things. Sometimes your VW is a sex symbol, and sometimes it isn't (Rosenbaum, 1972). Designer labels are presige only in certain class subcultures; they are markers of tacky in others. The rejection of fashion labels is a prestige marker in some class groups. It may be that establishing ourselves in a hierarchy is a universal human trait, and prestige is one of the ways people arrange themselves in hierarchies.

## Prestige in perspective

People talk as if class were about money. People act as if class were about prestige. Sometimes this is to advertise their money through their purchases of positional goods. The social construction of prestige is a complicated dance among consumer, manufacturer, advertiser, and the consumer's real and perceived peer group. On campus this dance is among students looking for colleges, college admissions staff, those marketing college rankings, and the students' parents and peer group.

## Experience

Look at all your clothing and accessories, and assign a class value to each item.

Wear something totally outrageous, nonprestigious, or inappropriate (wear something gender bending, paint your face yellow, wear a stage moustache, etc.) and see how people interact with you, how people talk to you, and how that single thing dominates your day.

## Reflection questions

In what ways do you respond when you see something that is an obviously labeled fashion? What in you reacts this way?

## Discussion questions

Is it fair to group students based on their prestige fashions?
Is prestige just about money?
What does it mean when someone's clothing has no labels and he or she doesn't wear college names or logos?
What does it mean when someone, like Misty, wears only fashion labels?

What is the best phone and what is the most prestigious phone?

Is body weight part of prestige?

How have you used someone else's rankings to help you make a decision?

Do you feel fashion competitive?

# CHAPTER 12

# *Class as Occupation*

THIS COULD BE A subchapter about prestige, but occupation deserves specific mention. Research on occupational prestige is clear: Job titles stack up in a hierarchy. Davis et al. (1991) ranked 505 occupational categories based on participants' answers to a 1989 general social survey and developed a prestige score for each occupation. The scores ranged from 86 for physicians to 17 for miscellaneous food preparation occupations ("Would you like fries with that?"). The top three occupational categories are, not surprisingly, physicians (86), lawyers (75), and professors and teachers (74). Losing out to physicians is a source of tension on college campuses that leads to discussions about who are the "real doctors." Losing out to lawyers in prestige is an open wound among professors. The prestige rankings are just that, rankings. These rankings may reflect the research participants' idea that money and occupational prestige are equivalent. I have the impression that attributed income has a great deal to do with attributed occupational prestige, but I have found no data on that.

Hollingshead (1975) used occupational attainment ranked in order of prestige to generate a measure of social status using census codes for occupations and grouping occupations into nine categories. Each group is well defined by occupational codes, so his category of "lesser professionals" is well defined by occupational titles. The original publication, available in research libraries, lists each profession in each of the following nine categories:

Score 9: Higher executives, proprietors of large businesses, and major professionals

Score 8: Administrators, lesser professionals, proprietors of medium-sized businesses

Score 7: Smaller business owners, farm owners, managers, minor professionals

Score 6: Technicians, semiprofessionals, small business owners

Score 5: Clerical and sales workers, small farm and business owners

Score 4: Smaller business owners, skilled manual workers, craftsmen and tenant farmers

Score 3: Machine operators and semiskilled workers

Score 2: Unskilled workers

Score 1: Farm laborers/menial service workers

(Hollingshead, 1975, pp. 5–15)

There is no reason to believe there have been important changes in occupational prestige rankings since the 1989 data were collected by Davis et al. (1991) because those rankings correlated quite highly with Hollingshead's (1975) ranking. Changing a few points in occupational prestige rankings will hardly affect the overall scheme of occupational prestige. A change of a few points may be meaningful to someone in a particular occupational category, for example, professors in their quest for occupational prestige supremacy over lawyers, but among the large list of occupations the fine distinctions are washed out in light of the great range of occupational rankings.

A demonstration of the power of prestige in occupational rankings can be found among faculty who situate themselves in a hierarchy based on arcane principles of perceived prestige of disciplines and how close the discipline is to a real science or to one of the founding disciplines. This plays out on a campus with the relative rankings of departments and schools. The hierarchy values traditional academic disciplines like physics and devalues applied disciplines like education. The fight for prestige dominance between math and physics, between computer hardware departments and computer software departments is a spectator sport on campus. The fights are so vicious because the stakes are so low. A close look at any profession or occupational group will show fine-grain hierarchies among specialists.

Van Galen (2000) makes an interesting point about the ambiguity of the prestige of the teaching occupation. Many teachers are unionized, which aligns them with labor, which aligns them with the laboring classes. All teachers have a college degree and many teachers have graduate credits or degrees, which aligns them with the educated classes. Public school teachers are public employees, which aligns them with the service class. Teachers are authority symbols, which aligns them with the authority class. No wonder we in the United States are ambiguous about the social status of teachers.

The relationship between profession and income is interesting as the economy of the world changes. Physicians are making less money and teachers are making more money. Money may be replacing occupational prestige as a primary marker of prestige, so bankers and stockbrokers will ultimately have higher prestige than physicians and professors. The markers of prestige and class change, but class remains.

## Occupational prestige and social dominance

"What do you do?" is a ritual greeting in the United States. I argue that the primary purpose of this question is to establish everyone's place in a hierarchy of occupational prestige. What difference does it make to me if you are an aircraft mechanic, a diesel engine mechanic, or a rocket engine mechanic? While I can chat briefly about the advances in motors and rockets, the chances are good I have no need for the knowledge and skill represented by these professions. I don't own an airplane, a diesel motor, or a rocket, so why exchange occupational identities if not for occupational prestige hierarchy dominance?

"What's your major?" is a campus greeting ritual, and there may be utility in knowing other students' majors. "Hey, I've got a class with Barratt this semester and I am doing that case study. Can you give me any pointers?" As with work, knowing someone's major contextualizes other students in the hierarchy of prestige major dominance. Students in traditional college majors with no immediate vocational application, such as history and philosophy, have ambiguous campus prestige.

These "useless" majors are low prestige in certain circles and high prestige in others. Their value depends on the class subculture and the role of education in occupational choice. In the liberal arts/general education view of college, philosophy and history have high prestige, and criminology has low prestige. In the vocational education view of college, criminology has high prestige, along with accounting, nursing, and all the rest of the high-enrollment programs preparing students for a specific job, and philosophy and history have low prestige because they don't prepare students for employment as a philosopher or historian after graduation without further education.

## Occupations and class summary

While I prefer the individual view of class as a socially constructed identity, prestige is perhaps the best marker for social class. People talk as if class were money; people act as if class were prestige. Somehow prestige has become a marketable commodity that is independent of product quality. Prestige, like social class, is entirely made up. Exploring the world of prestige is exploring the world of the irrational. Harvard is the highest-prestige university in the United States and probably in the world. Why is this the case? Harvard is among the most highly selective universities in the world; it gets smart students from families with great social, cultural, and economic capital, which leads inexorably to massive endowments, which leads to more publicity. On the other hand, do students learn more during their career at Harvard than at a lower-ranked school? The best and the worst lectures I ever heard were at Harvard.

## Experience

As you meet new people, ask about their major or occupation and use class as a lens to pay attention to how you feel when you learn what they do.

## Reflection question

How important to you is the prestige of your chosen occupation?

## Discussion questions

With most occupations for people with a college degree ranked as high prestige is it fair to call college graduates middle class?

Why do people rank occupations by prestige?

In your classroom, use everyone's parents' job titles to rank occupations by prestige from 0 to 100. How much agreement is there in your class on these prestige rankings?

What is it about teachers' work that makes their prestige different from a professor's job prestige?

Are occupations divided into two or three groups by required education?

Are all manual labor jobs low prestige? What is the difference between working on an assembly line and being a surgeon since both require manual labor?

# CHAPTER 13

# *Class as Culture*

SOCIAL CLASS is a collection of subcultures arranged in a hierarchy of prestige.

Culture, like class, has multiple definitions. The underlying rationale for using culture to talk about class is that culture, like class, is a learned set of norms, values, behaviors, symbolic interactions, fashion sense, gender roles, food preferences, and all the other things we internalize as we grow up and become acculturated and develop our social class of origin identities, which is building cultural capital within that culture group. For Amy Tan in *The Joy Luck Club* (1989), the cultural capital chasm between her main characters is central to her story line. While each character has cultural capital, it is for a different culture. Much of the tension in the story comes from characters' applying their cultural capital in a totally different cultural setting. In a poignant scene in the film adaptation, a Western boyfriend adds soy sauce to a carefully prepared meal after the mother who cooked it, in a culturally appropriate self-effacing manner, minimizes her cooking ability and suggests the meal may need salt and flavor. Viewing class as a collection of socially learned norms, as a social identity, can help deconstruct class as culture on a more detailed level.

If class is a collection of subcultures arranged in a hierarchy of prestige, much like pearls on a strand, those subcultures, or pearls, nearer to you are more like your subculture and those more distant are less like you. Moving up a little or down in class along the pearls on the strand is moving into familiar territory. You know some people in the next subculture, the next pearl, and you know some of the norms, values, behaviors, symbolic interactions, fashion, gender roles, and food preferences of that next group. Moving two beads along the strand of pearls takes you into less-familiar territory, and you know a few people in that group. Moving five or six beads along the strand is foreign territory. Contacts with members of that subculture five pearls away are ritualized role performances for cross-culture contact that we learned in school, in court, in professional offices, in hiring people to paint the house, or in painting someone else's house.

Stereotypes of class reflect stereotypes of culture. What are poor people like? What are rich people like? What food does Louise eat? What food does Eleanor eat? These are all questions seeking generalizations about other people's cultures. Cultural generalizations are easy and insufficient answers. The stereotype that the underclass likes quantities of food, the middle class wants quality of food, and the upper class wants presentation of food is easy and insufficient. This stereotype is funny and, like many myths about class, partially true. Visit restaurants that cater to different groups on the hierarchy of prestige and weigh the food, taste the food, and look at the food. If you want to know what food people like, what fashion they like, how they manage symbolic interactions, ask them. Generalizing to any subcultural group, to any social class, quiets many of the authentic voices in that subculture or group. Some of Eleanor's peers have become physicians, some have become practicing attorneys, and some don't like vintage champagne or caviar or Brie. Some of Louise's friends who became physicians like Brie and caviar and not champagne.

## Subcultures and education

A good, simple, and insufficient example of class as cultural differences are these two statements from students about general education classes: "Why do I have to take this class? I'll never use this stuff." This reflects a utility and vocational view of education as useful. "Great, look at this, a class on Egyptian warfare! That sounds good." This reflects a general education view as personally developmental and intellectually stimulating. It is difficult to write about class as culture without making generalizations about the social classes. All generalizations are mostly true, and an exception does not make the generalization not true. An exception shows us the limits of generalizations. Ursula and Eleanor see college as developmental, as a place to experience. Ursula is preparing for a life of paid work, and Eleanor is preparing for a life of unpaid work.

*Etiquette.* The rules of etiquette provide a nice visual anchor to explore subcultural differences. Think about one-fork dinners, two-fork dinners, and three-fork dinners and you have a class generalization. You have a collection of etiquette norms arranged in a hierarchy of prestige. The fork rule works well in restaurants as a class assessment. If the two forks are the same size, the restaurant caters to diners who may be uncomfortable making distinctions between a salad fork and a dinner fork, much less between a dessert fork and a fish fork. Etiquette echoes Bourdieu's (1986) idea of embodied prestige cultural capital. Etiquette practiced by the prestige class is learned at home if, like Misty, Ursula, and Eleanor, you go to dinners requiring more than one fork.

Social class transition is a move between cultures akin to becoming bicultural. As with cultures, there are no clear boundaries between social classes. If an individual has cultural competence in a social class, that competence will extend to similar social classes but will not extend to dissimilar social classes. First-generation students attending a community college may have sufficient cultural competence to succeed in that environment. First-generation students attending a prestige college may not have sufficient cultural competence to succeed in that environment and will need to acquire appropriate cultural competence.

*Class, culture, and language.* We notice the Big Three when we meet people—gender, ethnicity, and class. Obvious gender cues are dress and physiology. Subtle gender cues about how you construct your gender come from behavior, conversation, and shared experiences. Obvious ethnicity cues are physical features. Subtle ethnicity cues about how you construct your ethnicity come from conversation and shared experiences. Obvious class cues are seen in fashion, language, and behavior. Recall Sherlock Holmes lecturing Watson on observing someone's clothing to determine the person's occupation. Recall how Twain described how Tom Sawyer, Huck Finn, and Becky Thatcher dressed. Recall how Sylvester Stallone and Vin Diesel use language in their working-class film roles. Subtle class cues about how you construct your class come from conversation and shared experiences.

Fashion is easy to change and language is hard to change. Dialects and varieties of English or French or German or whatever you speak as your first language are class ranked. We learn our language at home, in the neighborhood, and on the playgrounds in the context of our social class of origin. Pronounciation and vocabulary are class markers. Slang is a class marker, and different classes have different slang. Sentence structure is a class marker. Listen to recordings of President Franklin Roosevelt or President John Kennedy and pay attention to their variety of English, to their cadence, to their vocabulary. Pay attention to your reaction to how they speak. Listen to Tom and Ray Magliozzi on *Car Talk* and pay attention to their variety of English. Pay attention to your reaction to how they speak. Listen to a professor during class and pay attention to the variety of English and pay attention to your reaction to that variety of English. Strike up an out-of-class conversation with that professor and see if you get the same variety of English. Does a professor on campus play a different role in class, use a different variety of English, from what he or she uses in performing a hallway conversation role?

*Class, culture, and food.* Food preferences are basic to our social class of origin. "Why don't they have food here for people like me?" I heard this complaint at a national conference reception for faculty. The spread was great from my point of view. Wine, multiple kinds of cheese, dried salami, and crackers. From my colleague's point of view the Gorgonzola, the Brie, and the salami were inauthentic to his social class of origin. Comfort food is code for food from our youth, code for food from our social class of origin. Macaroni and cheese may be comfort food for you, and Brie on water biscuits may be comfort food for someone else.

The food selection in campus dining halls is the result of many decisions, and one of the factors in these decisions is what students eat.

If students don't eat the macaroni and cheese, it is served less often. If students finish all the vegetarian meals, those meals are served more often. The human aggregate, majority student dining patterns, is a major factor in setting the dining hall menus. After-hours food is another story. Late-night pizza costs money that Whitney Page and Louise don't have.

*Class, culture, and fashion.* Walk across your campus and look at the different fashion groups. Writers about student typologies comment on fashion as student type and membership markers. Art students are identifiable in dress and hairstyle. Fraternity and sorority students are identifiable in dress and hairstyle, as well as by the ever present Greek letters on their clothes. Student athletes are fashion identifiable. Students from the working, laboring, farming classes are fashion identifiable. Students from the upper classes are fashion identifiable. Different campuses have different arrays of fashion identifiable groups. On some campuses hoodies and shirts advertise stores found in a mall. On other campuses no labels on clothing is the rule.

## Cultures in competition

Belonging to a group means you identify with that group in some way. Orientation staff work hard to enculturate students and make them members of campus communities. Campus is a place of shared experiences like sports, concerts, classes, lectures by guest speakers, and the like, and shared rites of passage like orientation, first-year experiences, declaring a major, graduation, and shared symbols of membership like college wear. Campus membership, like class, is supposed to be exclusive. Membership on one campus means you are not a member of another campus. Membership in one class means you are not a member of another class. However, many students transfer from one campus to another, so they have multiple campus memberships.

Most of us have different group memberships for our different interests. Some of our memberships are strong—for example, a major—and some of our memberships are weak—a group of basketball friends, for example. Class membership is very strong, and dual-class membership is like being a Yankees fan and a Red Sox fan. We are us, they are them. This pressure to be monocultural makes life difficult for Whitney Page and Louise. They are encouraged to join a new class group and leave their social class of origin group.

Interclass conflict is a way to reinforce your class membership and establish dominance for your class over my class. Members of Louise's class will see Misty as morally inferior because Misty doesn't have to work hard and has been given everything. This sense of moral superiority reinforces the value of Louise's subculture and reinforces the low value of the upper classes. When and if Louise changes in her current felt social class or her attributed social class to Misty's class, Louise will internalize that sense of moral inferiority that she has felt toward Misty. She will internalize class conflict.

## Student cultures, student typologies

A number of student typologies are ways of grouping students by common characteristics. Readers can readily identify the student groups on their campus. The typical list includes fraternity and sorority students, athletes and fans, the studious, the politicians, geeks, popular students, partiers, aggies, preppies, commuters, and so on. Some groups are campus specific and some groups are found on many different campuses. Each group will have its own ideas of prestige, cultural capital, and social capital. Each group will arrange a hierarchy of groups, placing themselves and others in the collection of subcultures arranged in a hierarchy of prestige.

Astin (1993) used a 60-item questionnaire and Q factor analysis to empirically identify eight types of students on campus. My bias is toward empirically based models even though Astin doesn't include my favorite student groups: geeks and nerds. He named each group according to some defining characteristic: Scholars, Social Activists, Artists, Hedonists, Leaders, Status Strivers, Uncommitted, and No Types. The names pretty much say it all for seven of the eight. Seven of these groups are typical college students of some variety. Astin described students in the eighth, or No Type, group in the following:

Students who failed to qualify as one of the seven types come from families with less education and lower incomes than any of the types. They also have by far the lowest degree aspirations and, except for the Hedonists, the poorest academic records from high school. The No Type students were also less involved in leadership and extracurricular activities during high school than any of the seven types. They infrequently studied with other students and were seldom guests in teachers' homes. No Type students are heavily concentrated in community colleges and underrepresented in public universities and all types of private institutions. (p. 44)

Is there a better description of Whitney Page or Louise or their siblings, or of first-generation students? Astin (1993) successfully identified first-generation students in his typology. The class bias in the 60 questions Astin used reflects the reality of Misty's, Ursula's, and Eleanor's lives. The class bias in describing college students selectively excludes first-generation students so they get identified as No Type. The 60 items are all about consuming college in ways that confirm class.

## Faculty cultures, faculty typologies

Students seem to be more interesting than faculty for researchers to classify so there are no empirical typologies for faculty. As a surrogate for faculty typology we can use the classic three areas of faculty work: research, teaching, and service. Faculty members and administrators at research institutions like TFSU worship at the altar of funded research. Arcane research is perceived at that campus as good, and applied research is suspect. Teaching is a clear second place to research at these institutions, and service is simply something that must be done. At small, selective liberal arts colleges teaching is paramount and research is second. Teaching is typically taken seriously in faculty reviews at smaller schools.

Prestige journals, the arbiters of prestige research, are highly selective and have a reputation as prestigious because nearly everyone at research universities regards them as prestigious. Publishing in prestige research journals is the coin of the realm for faculty members to succeed in the dominance and hierarchy contests on campus. Publication in prestigious journals is a form of academic capital that proves faculty prestige. Tenure review committees have been known to weight journal articles by the prestige of the journal. Applying Bourdieu's (1986) analysis of the reproduction of class, perceived prestige research journals are examples of the mechanism of the reproduction of class and of the intellectual paradigms held sacred by the journal editors and authors.

This book will actually count against my academic capital because it is applied and almost readable. Had I written a boring, flat review of everything everyone else had written on class, the book would be interesting to a few scholars, and I would receive great academic capital. The number one criticism of this book from faculty colleagues will be that it is not scholarly. It is not a review and reproduction of existing ideas.

As faculty members we have two jobs. First, we are conservators of all that has come before to which we add an occasional drip to the bucket of knowledge. Second, we are supposed to be out there on the edge coming up with new and radical stuff. Guess which one has more prestige (read higher class) on campus among faculty members, reproduction or production?

## The reproduction of culture

A group of Polish immigrants in Chicago lived securely in a Polish neighborhood. It was a comforting ethnic bubble reinforcing Polish culture, norms, gender roles, values, food choices, music, and all things Polish. The immigrants also lived in insecurity, afraid that someone would infiltrate their bubble, that some outsider would contaminate their bubble, that other norms would be on display. People in gated communities live in fear of the outside infiltrating their secure bubble. The gates can be cultural, physical, psychological, or college admissions standards, but people do live in gated communities and bubbles as a way to preserve and reinforce their system of ethnic and class exclusivity, surrounded by the values, foods, music, and culture of their choosing.

## Class, culture, privilege, and oppression

Peggy McIntosh (1988) developed a wonderful list of White privilege that has led other scholars to explore privilege as a list of specific behaviors and social interactions. Alimo, Washington, and MacDonald-Dennis (2003) explored Christian privilege expanding on the work of McIntosh. Other privilege lists have emerged, and a Google search will reveal many of them.

Privilege and oppression are transactional. While there are demographic characteristics, for McIntosh (1988) Whiteness and maleness that lead to privilege is the interpersonal transaction that grants privilege and creates oppression. Privilege and oppression are interpersonal acts, not abstract analytical concepts. You oppress me. I oppress you. You privilege me. I privilege you. Privilege and oppression are abstract notions used as an analytical tool. When they are used abstractly they obscure the idea that individual actions are the source of privilege and oppression.

Privilege and oppression are by-products of any cohesive group. Any group of people that has boundaries, members, and nonmembers will privilege members and oppress nonmembers. Members of groups with resources create structural and organizational ways of oppressing nonmembers who seek access to those resources. Voter registration requirements were one way those with power and resources created structural methods to oppress those without power. Landownership, the ability to read, gainful employment, and other structural barriers have been used to prevent citizens from voting.

## Summary

Culture is complex. The simple model here is that culture is a common set of values. The 60 items that make up Astin's (1993) research instrument are a very limited model of culture, and one that is biased toward second-generation students. The point is that even such a simple 60-item model reveals the classed nature of the collection of subcultures on campus that are arranged in a hierarchy of prestige. Achieving cultural competence in two worlds is exceptionally difficult for Whitney

Page and Louise. Achieving awareness of culture is exceptionally difficult for Misty. Ursula and Eleanor have always lived in culturally different worlds and have cultural competencies in different class and national cultures. Ursula's becoming culturally competent in Mexico did not diminish her cultural competence in her culture of origin. Whitney Page's and Louise's becoming culturally competent in the dominant campus class culture often comes at the expense of their cultural competence in their social class of origin.

## Experience

Visit your campus or local fine art museum or art gallery and pay attention to your feelings, your mood, and your reactions to the art and to the experience. The knowledge to consume art, or appreciate art, is one form of cultural capital, and many people don't feel comfortable in museums because they lack the cultural capital to appreciate the collections.

## Reflection question

How comfortable are you with what you know about art when you go to a fine art museum?

## Discussion questions

If culture is shared attitudes and beliefs, how do the faculty and administrators and staff on your campus try to shape your attitudes or beliefs?

How are the food selections on your campus a reflection of class?

How is your campus curriculum designed to provide students with cultural capital of the prestige social class?

How is the cultural capital of the lower classes negatively sanctioned or excluded on your campus?

How much do you value cultural capital or being cultured?
Can you learn to be cultured?
Is being in one of the student groups a cause or an effect of being
cultured?

Which student groups on your campus, for example, athletes, Greeks,
or art majors, most value prestige cultural capital?

# CHAPTER 14

# *Class, Ethnicity, and Gender*

## More Complexity

THIS CHAPTER is more about questions than answers. Because generalizations about class, gender, and ethnicity are suspect, the questions here are intended as opportunities for personal reflection. The answer to "What are working-class men like?" is so general it's useless. The answer to "What is your experience of gender and working-class men?" is yours alone and should serve as a starting point for your exploration of class and gender.

### Class and gender

Members of different social classes have different ideas about gender. Members of different genders have different ideas about class.

Stereotypes are an easy way to identify cultural norms. Actors Vin Diesel, John Wayne, Charles Bronson, Clint Eastwood, and Sylvester Stallone have all portrayed working-class men in a similar way. Sean Connery, George Lazenby, Roger Moore, Timothy Dalton, Pierce Brosnan, and Daniel Craig have all portrayed James Bond in a similar class way. Marlon Brando portrayed Stanley Kowalski in *A Streetcar Named Desire* as an underclass brute. Jackie Gleason portrayed Ralph

Kramden in *The Honeymooners* as almost a brute. Henry Fonda portrayed Tom Joad in *The Grapes of Wrath* as a meek and mild-mannered family man. There are multiple models of men in the underclass. Are the female leads in those epics the femininity stereotypes for the underclass woman?

The original *Guess Who's Coming to Dinner* (Kramer, 1967) may be the last great movie about upper-class men and women in their natural habitat. Jim Backus's portrayal of Thurston Howell III and Natalie Schafer's portrayal of Eunice "Lovey" Howell in *Gilligan's Island* (Schwartz, 1964–1967) forever created a stereotype for upper-class masculinity and femininity. This comic portrayal is funny because it is an underclass image of the upper-class gender stereotypes.

## Class and ethnicity

Members of different classes have different ideas about ethnicity. Members of different ethnicities have different ideas about class.

There are too few films to illustrate these points. A wealthy African American will appropriately have a different idea about class than a wealthy Chinese American or a wealthy European American. The meaning of class is individually created and grounded in how we each became acculturated in our ethnicity.

## Class, gender, and ethnicity

So what does a third-generation Indian immigrant from Chennai, daughter of two physicians, think about anyone else's social class? The exploration of the interrelationships among class, gender, and ethnicity is complicated. One decision is to determine how important each of the Big Three (class, gender, and ethnicity) is to the matter under discussion. This goes back to the screwdriver problem. Which tool is needed for this problem? Sometimes gender should be the primary concern. Sometimes ethnicity should be the primary concern. Sometimes class should be the primary concern. Much of the text here has put class up front in the discussion as a way to foreground the role of class. This is not to argue that class is more important or less important than any other characteristic of diversity.

To decide the importance or worth of a particular socially constructed identity in relation to another particular socially constructed identity I rely on the advice of Cseresnyesi Lazlo, whom I asked to compare life in Hungary to life in the United States: "It's not better, it's not worse, it's just different" (C. Lazlo, personal communication, 1984).

## Experience

Listen to men and women from different ethnic groups about what they believe about class.

## Reflection questions

What do you believe about gender roles for college-educated men and women or even men and women with graduate degrees? What are the women supposed to be like and what are the men supposed to be like?

What do you believe about gender roles for men and women who don't have a high school diploma? What are the women supposed to be like, and what are the men supposed to be like?

## Discussion question

What is the difference between what lower-class women like Whitney Page or Louise believe about women and gender and what Ursula and Eleanor believe about women and gender?

# CHAPTER 15

## *Stories*

WHILE WHITNEY PAGE, LOUISE, MISTY, URSULA, ELEANOR, and all the other characters in this book are based on real people and real events, they are fictional and were created to illustrate specific points. The following are class autobiographies. I sought out volunteers who were not European American women to provide the background for these stories and to bring a variety of voices and experiences into the discussion.

## ZACH'S STORY

My first awareness of my own social class came when I was entering high school and my parents divorced. Until that point I had lived a comfortable middle-class life in the suburbs of New Hampshire where both my parents worked and provided for my brother and me. We did not have an overabundance of money before the divorce but were able to go on vacations from time to time, and we had money for additional expenses like the travel soccer clubs that my brother and I were a part of. We also had pets as we grew up. I now understand pet ownership on a personal level as a marker of financial privilege.

After my parents divorced my brother and I lived primarily with my mother. While she was able to give us what we needed, the comfort of our previous lives disappeared. We never went on a vacation with our mother. Whenever we needed new clothing or something that would be an additional expense we were told to ask our father for it. While I never felt I had to worry if I would be able to eat in the evening, food options were limited and we had a basic amount of food in the house. I can remember after the divorce applying for scholarships to play on the expensive club soccer team we had joined. After the divorce and as we got older we were encouraged to name our mother as our main source of income when filling out financial aid forms so we could get the maximum amount of aid to attend college.

In thinking about my transition to college, my choice of where I would attend school was motivated by finances, and it was a choice not made by me but by my father. I was granted a substantial academic scholarship, half tuition for all four years, totaling $60,000, to a small, private liberal arts college on the East Coast. I had wanted to go to school in Colorado, but my father told me that if I wanted to go to a different school, I would be on my own in paying for college, for airfare to and from school, and for any additional expenses that may come up during the course of my matriculation. I can recall sitting up at night at a friend's house with my friend's mother trying to see if it would be worth it to attend the orientation session at the school in Colorado. My friend's mother said she would go to the orientation with me if I wanted. I was touched and confused by this statement. I didn't understand how my family, and specifically my father, would not support me in the same way my friend's mother was doing. At the time, I was unaware of the financial hardships my father was going through after the divorce. He had lost his job after the divorce and drained his savings before getting another job. He did not share this with my brother and me for fear that we would feel responsible for his financial crisis or that he would appear to be a father who was unable to provide for his children.

I was having a hard time dealing with how money would be a barrier to my getting what I so desperately wanted at the time, as it had not been a barrier in the past. Not that I was spoiled or lived a life of opulence, but I was able to do the things I wanted to do to blend in and be a happy kid growing up. This new approach to social class seemed counterintuitive in a way that I was having a hard time processing.

While my awareness of money and social class certainly increased as a result of my parents' divorce, I also gained further awareness of my class because of the working-class value of having to work hard to pay my way. In addition I was a second-generation Italian American whose immigrant grandfather talked about having to work three to four jobs most of his life to support his four children and wife. I remember being told when I turned 15 that it was time for me to find a summer job, which was my introduction to the life of work. Work at a young age was seen as the normal way of life in my family. Instead of having a summer of leisure, camp, or spending time and money, I was told it was time to earn my own money and pay for any extras I may want. I no longer received an allowance, which was perhaps $10 a week at the most, and I learned through my job the value of hard work and earning my own paycheck. I can remember having to fill out tax paperwork as a 16-year-old and my father telling me to try and work through the forms on my own. He apparently wanted me to become self-sufficient. Tax preparation became a yearly event that, while not overly difficult, always left me with the same feeling toward my father. I wanted to say to him: "I get that you are trying to teach me something, Dad, but I would really just like some help now."

This feeling of wanting help also manifested itself when I saw other people living a life of comfort and ease. This happened often at college, where I worked multiple jobs each year for spending money. My friends received allowances from their parents, but if I wanted money I needed to earn it on my own. I never could ask my parents for money because my mother did not have any, and if my father did, he wasn't going to give it to me. I spent a lot of time and energy trying to make money or cover up the fact that I did not have as much as my friends and people around me. Because I went to a small college where most everyone knew each other I can remember feeling the need to cover up my lack of money. I tried to do this by watching what I wore and presenting an image of myself as someone with disposable income. I can recall always looking forward to payday but never being able to save money as most of it went to books or to more frivolous expenses like dinners, movies, and clothes. I felt as though I were caught in a trap. I could not save because I wanted to present an image of being wealthier than I was, but also I was not able to become wealthier because of my inability to save. It was a cycle I was not aware of at the time. Looking back on my college years I am glad this cycle did not consume me as much as it could have. I never succumbed to credit card debt, and I continued to feel that if I just worked a little harder, if I could spend a few more hours at work or find another job, then maybe I would be in a better place when I graduated.

I remember the week I was set to graduate and I went looking for a car. I had my heart set on a Volkswagen Jetta, a decision based not on fiscal responsibility but more on my desire to have a German-made car as a sign of affluence and status. I found a Jetta TDI at a dealer, and after I took it for a test-drive I fell in love. I had to have that car. I gathered my courage, and from the kitchen of a friend's apartment I called my father to ask him for some help in making a down payment. I remember our conversation as if it happened yesterday. When I finally asked my father if he would be willing to help me out, he said no, and then he told me to "have fun with the payments." I remember getting the car partially to spite him and show him I could do it myself, all the while knowing that some of my peers were getting thousands of dollars and other extravagant gifts for graduating right alongside me. Once again the jealousy of not having money in the same way that others around me had money debilitated me and fueled a sense of anger and contempt. Why wasn't I able to have the same comforts others had? Did I not work hard enough? When would my day come? Would it ever? And after all the questioning and self-doubt, I had to settle on the fact that I was doing it on my own, fending for myself, able to provide for myself in a way that others my age did not understand or were unable to do. In a way, I created a sense of entitlement about my working-class background that protected me from the fact that I had less than others around me, thus making me less self-conscious and less hurt about my social class standing.

When I moved to the Midwest to go to graduate school, I began to realize that privilege came with my growing up in the Northeast, and I began to understand the implications of my desire to mask my social class in front of other people. I can remember having a conversation with classmates during my second year of graduate school about social class, and one of my peers seemed shocked when I told her about my family and what my life was like when my parents got divorced. She told me that for the past year she had just assumed I came from old money because I was from the Northeast. Her comment made me think not only about the regional differences in our country—she had grown up in the Southeast and settled in the Midwest—but also about the way I presented myself to others. I can remember having a difficult time with her comment for weeks after she made it, feeling guilty and ashamed of myself for having to mask who I was and my working-class roots. I became frustrated with myself for not being comfortable in my own skin and immediately saw that much of what I used to cover my social class—my clothes, my car, and my inability to save money because I was going out more often than I should have—was an empty and shallow waste. This guilt, however, was not enough to change my behavior or spending habits.

If during my youth I was unaware of social class, and college was a time of self-consciousness and frustration over not having more money compared to my peers, graduate school marked another transition in my understanding of social class, specifically in relation to the privileges I had associated with social class. I began to realize that because of my level of education, I was a part of a select group of people who would be able to advance easier and make more money over a career. In addition, I began to understand the insidious nature of privilege, namely, the intersections of the dominant dimensions of personal identity I had as a White man. I would make more money, receive a loan should I ever want one, and even be seen as being more wealthy than I actually was because of these dominant identities. Much of these realizations came from volunteer work I did at a local extension center for a community college in a rural town outside Macomb, Illinois, where I attended graduate school. This other town, Bushnell, was incredibly poor. I remember my supervisor telling me over 90% of the residents were below the poverty line. One of the first times I drove there, I can remember thinking about how lucky the residents were to have the extension center where they could educate themselves and set themselves up for success. I was still under the illusion that if only they worked hard enough, they would be able to lift themselves out of poverty. My turning point came when a student named Scott came in to speak with my supervisor. He had just gotten out of jail for the second time and had been out of jail for a week and had not seen his wife and two children yet. He was told by his boss that he no longer had a job, and he did not have a place to sleep because he had worn out his welcome with a friend of his that morning. He came to speak to my supervisor about wanting to take classes again so that he had something to hold on to, something to give him hope. He also wanted to get some money to rent a campsite so he would have a place to sleep for the next week, as he did not think his wife would want to see him. At one point during this conversation, I can remember my supervisor asking, "Scott, I am so sorry for asking, but can you remind me how old you are again?" His response was 23, the same age as me. On the ride home I called my partner at the time and almost broke down crying. What if I had been born in Bushnell? What if I had been born in worse circumstances? A lot of my social class standing had nothing to do with working hard or earning anything, but more about where I started in life, and while I did not start at the head of the class, I certainly had a substantial lead on Scott right out of the gate. Hearing Scott's story was the first time I realized that there was no single starting line where everyone began, but that starting lines were different depending on a number of factors. Being a White man who grew up in the Northeast in a middle-class family set me apart and gave me a boost without my having to do any work at all. I didn't earn my privilege—it was just handed to me.

Knowing what I know now about social class and privilege I now realize that I am lucky. While I do not have a lot of disposable income, I do recognize that I have a dog, am able to save some money, and can afford things like plane tickets to visit my family who live on the other side of the country. I also know I can enjoy going out from time to time without perpetually worrying about every penny. I still do not have credit card debt, but I own a car and enjoy leisure activities like a gym membership, cycling, and taking a graduate course at the college where I work. I equate these activities with those who have disposable income and who are able to spend money on activities. I realize I do not need to spend extra time at a second job to afford what I want but don't need. While I have often thought of getting a second job, I do not have to do so.

I still struggle with feelings of inadequacy in terms of how much money I have. I feel like Sisyphus rolling a stone up a mountain only to have it roll down to the bottom, requiring me to start over when I think of how much money I have in my savings account. However, I remind myself that I have a savings account and a retirement account, two things that not many others have. I also have a lot of years ahead of me, and I am nowhere near my earning potential at this point in my career. It is hard to not buy into social messages about what designer brand clothes I should wear, what kind of foreign-made sports coupe car I should drive, or even what sort of upmarket groceries I should buy. I try to quiet my vanity and remember that I am in control of my own life and I am doing just fine. I have made a lot of progress in terms of doing more with less and being able to save money. I have also been able to stop fixating on money as much as I have in the past, which has been liberating for me and has reduced my stress level significantly. Despite these developments, I know I still have a long way to go in my understanding of social class and how that affects and influences me; but perhaps knowing this is half the battle.

## KHOU'S STORY

When I was in K–12, I considered myself to be a part of the lower social class. My parents were born in Laos and came to the United States as refugees from Thailand because of the Vietnam War and the Secret War in Laos. My parents never finished grade school and were considered illiterate when they arrived in the United States. My father was sponsored by a family who took him in and showed him how to live in the United States, teaching him the basics of communicating in English. My mother and her family were sponsored by a Catholic church. My parents met in Richmond, California, and have seven children. I don't know all the details, but my father ended up working on the assembly line for Hewlett-Packard (HP) in Santa Rosa, California. He worked for HP for almost 20 years and opted for early retirement when the company closed that plant. My mother was a stay-at-home mom until I was about 16, and she had the duties of a typical housewife, making sure that the children were taken to school on time, picked up from school, and that dinner was ready for the whole family. With just my father working there was only one income to support the whole family, which meant my family was on a strict budget. At the end of my father's career with HP, he was making about $14 to $15 an hour. He currently works as an automobile technician at Walmart doing things like basic oil changes and lubes. My mother works for JCPenny as a seamstress for special-order items like curtains.

I remember as a child the best treat for me was the beginning of the school year because it meant I would get new clothing. We would typically go to Kmart because it had the best deals. I remember one year my father's coworker had given my parents a $100 gift certificate to a local used store, sort of like Goodwill, and everyone was so excited because $100 to our family was a lot of money. I remember I got some new clothes to add to my wardrobe even if they were used. Now when I think back, I see how poor we were and how the simplest things lit up my day.

As a poor family, during the holiday season we would get free food from charitable organizations, and it was always fun to help my parents unpack and see what kind of goodies were in the bags. Since my family didn't celebrate the traditional American holidays, we would get free toys at school during the Christmas holiday. I think I always somehow knew we were poor. From the time when I was a child, my parents always stressed to my siblings and me the importance of getting an education so we could live a better life than what my parents gave to us. It has always stuck with me, and I believe that is why I have such high ambitions for myself, because I want to give my parents and my family what they couldn't give us.

As I said earlier, I have always known I was bound for college even though I came from an uneducated family. Thinking back to how I prepared for college is hazy, and I don't remember the full details of how I knew what to do to apply for college. Since my parents had never attended college or did not know how to help me, I believe I surrounded myself with friends who came from the same social class as I did who had the same ambitions of obtaining a bachelor's degree. I did not do the college tour of universities and did not meet with admissions counselors to see what each university could offer me. I was pretty set on attending Sonoma State University (SSU), the local university, because as a child we always passed by it and I told myself that one day I would attend that university, which I did. It was the only university I applied to besides the local junior college, which was a backup. When I finished high school, my overall GPA was about 3.7. I was accepted to SSU and went in with honors.

In high school I remember the only counselors who came to visit my high school were the counselors in the Educational Opportunity Program (EOP) at SSU. They met with interested graduating seniors who wanted to go to college and helped us prepare our Free Application for Federal Student Aid. They also helped us apply for a grant in case we were interested in attending SSU. One of the great things my high school offered was a career center. We had a career counselor who knew a lot about higher education, and I remember spending a majority of my senior year in the center. The sad thing is that last I heard it was no longer there because of funding issues. I attended Elsie Allen High School, located on the southwest side of Santa Rosa, which is considered lower social class with students mainly of ethnic minorities. My high school was considered to be the worst high school with the lowest test averages. I guess you can say I speak highly of my high school because I came from there and I have achieved a lot, but then again I was always in the top 10% of my class.

I had filled out my application to SSU in early December, but did not hear anything until late April. I remember being scared and unsure of what my future held for me because it was the only university I applied to, and I could not fathom why it would not accept me. By then I knew my ethnic minority and class standing was an advantage to me, but I was still worried. One of my best friends and two close friends were accepted to SSU, and we all decided to room together to help us with the transition. I have to say, if I did not have my friends, I think SSU would have been a scarier place for me.

The summer of 2001 was life changing for me. I graduated from high school, got engaged, got disowned by my family because of my engagement, and went off to college. I was accepted for EOP at SSU and had to attend a summer bridge program. One of the main reasons EOP exists is to help low socioeconomic students succeed in college by offering services and grants to students who fit the profile. This program has been one of the best programs I have experienced in my life. After going through my family troubles, I almost dropped out of college because of depression, but somehow I found the strength to move forward because I had worked too hard to get where I was and I was not going to throw it away. I remember attending summer bridge and not wanting to be there, but I still participated in the activities. At the end of the program, I had made new friends and found a new family to replace the one I had lost. With the help of this program, I was better prepared for college. The staff helped me register for classes and figure out where I was going to live, and put me in a University 101 course to learn how to navigate college. Since my parents did not know how to help me, the university took the place of my parents. The EOP office became a frequent place for me to hang out and talk about my issues outside school. The staff helped me to mature and grow into a young lady.

Since I was estranged from my family, the first day was a stressful day. My fiancé and I showed up with my meager belongings, and it took less than an hour to move everything in. I lived in an eight-person apartment suite with four bedrooms. I roomed with my best friend and was neighbor to my two other close friends. The four other suitemates were from all over California. One was from Los Angeles, an only child from a well-off Jewish family. One came from Sacramento, the eldest of two and from I would say a middle-upper-class family. Another, from Vacaville, came from a middle-class family, and the last one was from Sonoma and was maybe from the same social class as I. I remember I was excited to meet them all but also scared. I remember that my suitemates from Sacramento and L.A. had a lot of belongings; their parents brought so many things into the rooms. They also took them grocery shopping and filled up their pantry with food. I remember I had wished my parents were there to help me move in and buy me food.

Since I attended the EOP summer bridge program, I knew at least 80 other students who were in the same boat as I was, and on occasion some of us would get together to eat at the dining hall and hang out. I felt comfortable at SSU and was lucky I did not feel too awkward when it came to social gatherings. Being in class was a different story. I think I have always felt a divide between the majority of my classmates and myself because of my social class standing and ethnicity. I believe it was my sophomore year at the beginning of the school year, and I was buying new clothing. I had asked my fiancé if the way I dressed looked like I was poor or middle class. It's funny how I can remember that exact day and what was on my mind. I wanted to fit in with my college classmates because most of them came from middle- to upper-class families.

I came to college without a car because I couldn't afford one, but a lot of the students who lived on campus had very nice vehicles that I could only dream of owning even to this day. I was usually one of two or three in my classes who were people of color and probably of lower social class standing. It always bothered me, and I felt the others were better than me because not only were they White, but they were wealthy as well in my eyes.

I remember my suitemates would go and have dinners off campus or do things and would invite me, but I would usually decline because I couldn't afford to go and also did not know how to budget my finances. I think that is one of the biggest challenges I had to get used to, budgeting my own finances, which I did horribly in college.

My parents never taught me how to budget, and I had to teach myself and learn the hard way. No one told me about credit cards and how they functioned. I remember when I would get my refund check for my financial aid, I would treat myself to an expensive outfit because I normally could not afford it and I wanted to show off that I had money too when I really didn't.

I remember during summer bridge we played a game about privilege and social class in which people took a step forward if they had a certain privilege. I remember being one of the last people in the back of the room and got teary eyed because I hated the fact that I came from a poor family and knew it and couldn't do anything about it.

One of the things I remember disliking the most about college was the care packages. When students were getting their care packages from their families I remember thinking to myself how I hated those packages because I knew I would never get one in the mail. For one, my parents did not know about care packages, and two, they couldn't afford to pay for one. Also being a part of EOP was looked down upon because students who were not a part of EOP saw it as a program for students who were poor and had low grades and were accepted only because of special circumstances. I remember I would have to tell people how you can have good grades and be a part of EOP because I was one of them. I think at one point in my college career I didn't want to be associated with EOP because of the assumptions other students had about it, and I didn't want them to know I was in EOP and needed the grant money.

As I think about social class today, I honestly don't know where to place myself. I have obtained a master's degree and am shocked to know that I am a part of the top 10% in social class standing, but I don't see myself in that way—or do I? I know I am more educated than most people I am affiliated with and maybe have not fully grasped or understood my new social class standing. Since graduating with my master's, a couple of people seemed awed and proud to know me because I have a master's, but to me it's something that is attainable and within reach. I guess to them it is impossible and something they will only dream of, which is kind of sad. I have noticed one of my close friends hasn't really congratulated me, and I wonder at times if it is because of envy or jealousy. I know my social class standing is a level above my family's background, but is it? My parents did not have any debt when I was growing up and were able to save money, but I have debt, yet I am more educated, so does that make me higher in social class standing? These questions come to mind and maybe it is something I need to research and study more, but what really consists of social class?

I guess I can say I live in a bicultural bisocial class world because I can relate to those who are from a lower social class but can also relate and know how to converse with those from the middle and upper classes. But when I look in the mirror at the end of the day, I still see and feel like a poor Hmong girl who is more educated than her parents but not wealthier. But then again, I know that my social class standing is higher than most of the people I know from back home. Maybe once I figure out my debt, I will feel more like I belong in the higher social class I am now a part of.

## CHRISTINA'S STORY

I am a first-generation African American woman with a graduate degree, and other than college and graduate school, I've lived in Sacramento my whole life.

According to a 2007 article in *Time* magazine, Sacramento is one of the nation's most diverse cities. I can attest to that as far as race is concerned. As a teenager, I'd walk around the local shopping mall and think nothing of seeing people in mixed-race relationships, people from different countries. However, diversity does not imply inclusivity or integration.

When people from Sacramento meet each other it's likely that one will ask the other, "Which part of Sacramento are you from?" The answer to this seemingly innocent question can tell you a lot about the resident. For example, if the reply is El Dorado Hills the resident lives in a very exclusive community. To put it bluntly: If you live in El Dorado Hills, you're rich. Sometimes an individual may say that he or she is from Natomas, for example, when the person actually lives in Rio Linda. This is because he or she does not want to be associated with the social class in Rio Linda, which is a poorer neighborhood, while Natomas is a booming suburb.

There are no true ghettos in Sacramento by definition. There are, however, many areas of the city where people from lower social classes live (the term *ghetto* is generally used when describing these parts of the city). In several areas of town you can tell the minute the social class of residents changes. It's almost as if an invisible line exists. From one street to the next the houses change shape and color and generally increase in size. The yards become much larger and are generally surrounded by black iron gates.

I lived down the street from Encina High School, but I always knew I would never attend that school. It was known for its substandard education along with the low social class of the students from the surrounding neighborhood. I went to El Camino Fundamental High School. To this day, I have no idea what the difference is between a high school and a fundamental high school.

In high school I rode the bus to and from school. Either because of the cost to the school or because of the low demand from students, there were no school buses available, so I took the city bus. The bus I took was popular among other students as well, and some of them moved to live down the street from my house so they could go to that school.

When I was old enough to drive, I received my mother's car. Well, we shared the car. She would walk to work and I would take her car to school. I took this same car with me to college. Any car repairs were paid by me, including an $800 brake job.

In my search for colleges, I didn't really know what to look for. I soon realized that the price tag was an issue and settled on a school that was part of the California State University system. Each semester of classes was less than $2,000, which was about the best I could do at a public university in California.

My aunt took me shopping for a few necessities about three days before I was scheduled to leave. I didn't buy much, partially because

I didn't want my aunt to have to spend much money on me and partially because I didn't really know what I would need.

I packed my things in our car and headed off to college with my mother. When I checked into my room in the residence hall we stepped into a pink palace. My roommate, Jacquelyn, had already moved in, and her side of the room was covered with everything pink and princess. She had a mountain of pillows on her bed, picture frames with princess crowns on them, and a desktop computer hooked up to a printer. I didn't even own a computer. I had received a scholarship through my church for $1,000 and planned to use that money to buy a computer.

I started to unpack my belongings and soon realized I had left a few essentials at home, including my pillow and towels. I think the absence of my belongings was amplified by the presence of Jacquelyn's things. Later, I was given a pillow that Jacquelyn's parents had purchased for me.

Jac and I lived peacefully, as far as I was concerned, in our room and never had any disagreements. We had a shared refrigerator and had agreed that we would each take responsibility and take turns keeping it stocked. I had few demands for food—why spend extra money when I can eat at the dining hall? So I didn't mind replacing any of her food that I ate. The first time I went shopping I decided that I would stop eating so much of her food so that I wouldn't have to replace it. Four dollars for cheese? Five dollars for cereal? That could get expensive to replace. Considering I worked only about 15 hours a week at my job off campus, I had to save as much money as I could.

A few weeks into classes, Jac began gathering information about sorority recruitment. She was extremely excited about the idea of joining a sorority and asked me if I was going to be joining one. I replied that I was not. I had no idea about sororities besides what I had heard and seen through the media. Through her, I came to realize that a sorority had a cost associated with it. I put it out of my mind after that. I could hardly afford to get through the semester and I couldn't afford to take part in any cocurricular activities. I couldn't understand how she could afford all these things without a job.

I made friends with a man from Sacramento, and during winter break we both met up a few times to hang out. He came and picked me up from my house in his pickup truck that had been purchased by his parents. He came into my house and met my mother. On another occasion, I went to his house. The moment I walked up to the front door, I recognized the home for what it really was and how it was different from homes in my neighborhood. Christmas lights were strung up on the roof and along a fence. Lighted reindeer in various poses were strategically placed under a tree, which made the deer look as if they were grazing on grass. The front door was decorated with a wreath, and a three-foot-high Santa Claus character was positioned next to the door.

I rang the doorbell and was welcomed by his mother and stepfather. The inside of the house was nothing special, but I began to feel that my house was much more inferior to this one. I realized how dirty the carpet was in my house that was once forest green and how the walls with handprints, dirt, and crayon on it made the home so much less appealing. The mold growing on the windows in each room seemed that much more of a problem to me when comparing them to the windows I saw in his house. I felt like I didn't belong there.

My best friend in college and I had a lot in common when it came to social class. Or so I thought. Her mother worked as a hairstylist for a department store and made about $25,000 a year. Her father was unemployed. However, I felt comfortable in discussing financial woes with her, mainly because I knew she would be able to understand much better than my new male friend or my roommate. She was just as desperate as I was to find and keep a job while she was in school. She held several jobs throughout her college career. Her involvement on the softball team made it difficult for her to find a job that could be flexible with her practice and game schedule, but she made do. Her jobs, unlike mine, were as much a way for her to pay for school as they were a way for her to support her parents. We lived together for almost four years, and I was comforted in knowing that she had the same values about money as I did.

## KEN'S STORY

I was born and raised in a moderate-size city in Michigan. I am one of three children. My mother is Mexican, my father is Irish. My parents are divorced, they separated when I was six years old. My mother raised my siblings and me by herself with the help of government assistance. We were definitely lower class. Most of the people in the neighborhood I grew up in were on welfare too, so I really didn't notice that much when I was younger. We have an incredibly large extended family—my mother had 13 siblings, and I grew up with nearly 60 cousins! Almost all could be classified as lower class.

School was not highly valued where I grew up; however, it was an environment I thrived in. I always got good grades and I loved going to school, and my family was surprised that I did so well in school. My mother dropped out of high school when she was a teenager (although she did go back in her 30s to get her diploma). My father graduated from high school and attended community college, and that was the highest level of education attained by anyone in my entire family. Most of my aunts, uncles, cousins, and even my brother and sister had dropped out of high school. My maternal grandmother was illiterate. There weren't high expectations for education in my family, and there was very little knowledge about college. This is part of the reason the transition was so challenging—I didn't know what I didn't know.

I lived with my mother until I was 15 years old, after which I went to live with my father. I still did very well academically in high school. However, I really didn't know anything about the college application process. It never came up in the few conversations with my high school counselor. Registering for the ACT was more of an accident than an intentional step. My friends who were on a college prep track were registering and asked me why I hadn't done it yet. Fortunately, my scores were good, and colleges in Michigan and around the Midwest began sending me letters. I received scholarship offers from several schools, and other schools offered to waive application fees or granted early admission. This process brought me mixed feelings; I was excited that colleges were interested in me, but on the other hand, I had no idea how to apply. Mixed feelings are a good way to sum up my entire college experience.

Living with my father was certainly one of the biggest reasons I was able to get to college. When it came time to fill out those college applications, I remember him telling me, "Son, I have never done it before. But if we work on it together, I know we can figure it out." And that is exactly what we did. We went to McDonald's one afternoon, spread out all the application materials and tax information on a big table, and spent about three and a half hours filling out paperwork. We weren't sure if we did it right, but when the University of Michigan sent me an acceptance letter, there was no doubt. Dad had patience and he was supportive. He did not want me to miss out on this opportunity.

So I was accepted, but I still didn't know what was next. I had never heard of a college visit, so I didn't go on any. To say we had very little money was an understatement. We could not afford senior pictures, a class ring, or even the college admissions fee. I had to call the admissions officer and ask for it to be waived. A letter from Michigan explained when and where orientation was. My dad took the day off work and drove me to Ann Arbor. We even got lost on the way. He dropped me off with a fan and a pillow, and he reminded me that I had to find my own ride home, which was two and a half hours away. Like so many times before and after, I would rely on my social skills to help me acclimate and figure out what needed to be done. I would make fast friends with other students and ask them questions about things I didn't understand or that were completely novel. Listening to students who were more familiar with the process helped me understand things like assessment, academic probation, course packs, and meal plans. My ability to get along well with others enabled me to learn from others and not appear like a clueless fool doing it.

I leaned on social skills in so many of the areas that my peers had familiarity with (and probably didn't give much thought to). I never had a bank account of any kind before. When my scholarship check came I walked to the nearest bank and asked what to do. The bank staff showed me how to write checks and use an ATM card. Computers—yikes! We didn't have one in the house and I had very little exposure in high school. Word processing was shaky—I didn't know how to save a document, send attachments—and the Internet and e-mail were totally new to me. I became an expert at appealing to the inner teacher in my friends and classmates. "How do you . . . ?" was my way to learn about what I was not privy to in my surroundings growing up. I would ask people in a way that made them feel good about sharing the information or method, either by acknowledging their expertise or by feeding their altruism.

When school started in the fall, I did just fine in the classroom; school was still an environment in which I thrived. I was fortunate that my talents lent themselves very well to success in the classroom. I was also extremely determined to do whatever it took to make it in college. I realize now that I put an inordinate amount of pressure on myself to do well at Michigan. The worst thing in the world would have been to not make it. The funny thing was that the pressure was not coming from back home or from my peers. In their eyes I was already a success just by getting into college. This experience was very different from that of other students I spoke with at Michigan. They felt pressure from many places—parents who were professionals, competition from high-achieving peers, and fear of not getting the grades to get into the "right" graduate school. My pressure was all internal—generated by me. I felt that I needed to be a role model for my cousins. Because of that, failure was not an option. If the "smart one" in the family couldn't make it in college—who of them would?

And so I would stay up late nearly every night studying, making sure I made it to every class and to my professors' office hours when necessary. Despite being a very social person, I denied myself opportunities to socialize, opting instead to study. It made my first year in college a tough one because it literally was all work and no play. I didn't focus on making friends because my focus was on making it—period. Naturally, this pace was stressful and made me keenly aware of how much fun I was not having. What made it worse was that it seemed that everyone back home was having a great time, and I was missing out, opting instead to study chemistry until two in the morning. I didn't have a car, so I couldn't drive back when I wanted to. Lack of money kept long-distance calls to a minimum. The folks around me seemed to have disposable income and friends to spare. The situation made me question sometimes if all the hard work was worth it. What was it all for? At the time, I wasn't sure.

As the semesters passed, I was able to alleviate some of that pressure because it became obvious that I could cut it on campus. In fact, I was excelling in the classroom. Where I was not making much progress was in my choice of major and program of study. Simply put, I had no idea there were academic advisers we could talk with to help us choose classes and decide on a major. Even more embarrassing is the fact that the academic advising office was located in a building that I had at least four classes in. While other students knew about these services, I was pretty much in the dark. Thank goodness for the graduate student who had a temporary office in my residence hall. She was able to refer me to an adviser I established a relationship with that lasted for the remainder of my college years. This adviser was empathetic and informed. She listened to me and explained things such as concentration requirements, credit/no-credit courses, and graduation audits. She was more helpful than she might have realized. Still, it is painful to think that this meeting might not have happened if it weren't for a chance encounter with a graduate student.

What's worse is that I never discovered the career center while I was on campus. I didn't learn about this resource until after I had graduated—and I went back because I still didn't know what I wanted to do careerwise. There were so many things I missed out on because either I didn't know they existed, or I didn't know how to navigate the process, including internships, student activities, study abroad, and service learning. When other students had internships during the summer, I worked two jobs. I would have cherished the opportunity to study abroad, but it seemed almost as if this activity were reserved for wealthy students only. Nobody back home knew about these things, and I really didn't realize all the opportunities that I was missing, and how helpful some of these resources were.

Everything I have mentioned so far was no doubt a challenge, but the hardest thing about going to college was the impact it had on relationships with my family. Not only did going to school increase the physical distance between me and my family, it increased the emotional distance between us. I was experiencing so many new things at college, some of them very exciting and interesting, but when I tried to talk about these things with the folks back home, they didn't understand. Eventually I would just talk about different things and ask how people were doing. Over time, I would talk less and less to family. Because our family was so poor, no one could afford a car, making visits to campus almost nonexistent. That was hard because I wanted to show my family and friends all the great things about my school. I wanted to share those experiences with them. I can count on one hand the number of times *any* family member came to visit during my entire college career. Contrast this with my roommates whose parents came to visit regularly or sent care packages in the mail with snacks and "lucky exam socks." And of course, all my roommates had cars. It was sometimes embarrassing to ask them for rides home or to borrow the car because I couldn't reciprocate. These were all feelings I couldn't discuss with family because I didn't want them to feel bad or inferior by comparison.

The more I became acclimated to college, the farther apart I grew from my family. Without knowing it, I was changing. Subtle as they were, these changes were real and affected how I spoke, how I dressed, whom I hung around with, and they even started to affect my values. In essence, my social class was changing. In my mind and heart I still thought I was just a poor Mexican kid from Muskegon, lower (lower) class, trying to make it. But on the outside, I had adopted middle-class values and customs, and I did make it. The sacrifice was that I had to leave everyone behind to do it. And so my college experience is best summarized as mixed feelings. I am proud of my accomplishments, and I enjoy the opportunities and lifestyle my college education gave me. However, I have never reconciled the guilt I feel about living a better life while the people I care about the most still struggle with their social class issues.

# ABE'S STORY

Both my parents have PhDs from the University of Iowa. My mother is a university administrator, and her father was a physician. My father is a psychologist, his father was a barber, and his mother was a teacher and finished her college education along with my father, who was first in his family with a college degree. I have two sisters, older and younger, and older cousins who also went to college.

I saw our family as a middle-class, extremely supportive family and considered myself to be wealthy but certainly not rich. We had enough money to have everything we needed but not so much that we were spoiled. My father grew up with very little money, so he lived frugally and understood the value of money and saving. I used to do chores like pulling weeds at Dad's office building (of which he was part owner) to save money, and I had a quarterly clothing allowance, so I learned early that money wasn't endless. I also had a credit card early, and that taught me about the importance of spending responsibly and building good credit. I played many sports, was very active, and did well in school. In middle school I befriended an exchange student from South Korea who didn't speak any English, and I remain fascinated with other cultures.

In high school I didn't drink or get in trouble, and I was often gone from school playing soccer. I had many friends but not many close friends. Most of my very close friends were those I played soccer with in the Detroit area. I started playing seriously in eighth grade and gave up other sports because we had to drive between one and one and a half hours each way to practice. I often stayed overnight at teammates' houses for early morning practices and games on weekends. I had a personal coach who donated his time to train me on the days I didn't have practice, and I used to get up before school and practice early in the morning. I also used to do homework in the car on the way to practice in Detroit while Mom or Dad drove there from our home, and sometimes I got up early in the morning to finish assignments before school. I was a good student but never considered myself to be remarkably intelligent. I always thought I was pretty smart in high school, but there were plenty of students I thought were more naturally smart and worked harder in school.

As I got better and better at soccer and started making state, regional, and national teams, school became slightly less important because I knew soccer would differentiate me and allow me to get into better schools than I would with academics alone. I was an elite athlete, one of the best players in the country coming out of high school. I played on the best club team in the state and was very committed. For me life revolved around soccer: diet, practices, games, tournaments. It dictated my friends and my schedule. I ended up being good friends with middle- to upper-class White kids on my team from the Detroit area, most of whom had more money than I did but weren't as good players. I was captain of my team and had a great deal of social capital because of my playing ability.

I was offered and I accepted a soccer scholarship to Stanford University, and when I got there I was amazed at the accomplishments of my peers. I really wanted to experience something different from what I was used to. Going to school in California, far away from home, was exciting and I was excited to be somewhat out on my own rather than going to school in the Midwest where my parents were in driving distance to see me (and vice versa). I was humbled by fellow students and intimidated by their intelligence and accomplishments. My athletic scholarship covered 75% of my tuition and room and board; what my parents had saved for me covered the remainder of that. I did not need to take additional student loans to pay for college. Were it not for the athletic scholarship I would have needed to take on significant debt to pay for a school like Stanford.

At school I became extremely close to my fellow teammates, especially those in my incoming class. My roommate was a nonsoccer player, and we got along very well but didn't hang out much socially. Almost all my social activities were with my fellow teammates, perhaps because I felt more secure around them. Many, if not most, of the other students came from very wealthy families. Campus was pretty self-contained, and most social activities took place on campus, so people didn't go out much and there was not a lot of pressure to spend money. The main exception to that was when parents came to visit, and it was typical for them to take a handful of friends out to dinner. People would talk about their parents' taking a big group of students to fancy restaurants in Palo Alto, and I was often invited to go along, which made me feel some pressure to reciprocate when my parents came to visit. While they could afford to do this from time to time, I was a little uncomfortable feeling like they needed to.

Despite the fact that my primary expenses were covered, I felt like I wanted to have a little extra money to spend and not worry about being on such a tight budget, so I decided to work. I am also pretty thrifty, a trait I picked up from my dad, who grew up in a blue-collar family where money was scarce. I earned the nickname "Abe-Bay" because I would stock up on cheap, used dorm furniture at the end of the school year when everyone was trying to move out, then I would sell it back to people in the fall when they were moving back into dorms. This was made easier by the fact that my parents gave me the old family conversion van. I stored TVs, microwaves, and other similar items in the van over the summer, then delivered them to people in the fall. Working gave me something else that other people weren't doing. I felt like I was accomplishing something they weren't by juggling another thing on my schedule and making money while also playing soccer and going to school.

I started working as a cashier in the café at the business school during my junior year. I worked a range of 10 to 20 hours per week depending on my academic and athletic schedules. Having money coming in definitely made me feel more self-sufficient and less guilty if I wanted to buy new clothes or buy dinner. Having a car was stressful because people always wanted to borrow it. I felt uneasy with other people driving it, especially because it was such a big car and it was easy to hit curbs (or worse) if you had never driven it before. I was nervous that something would happen, and other drivers wouldn't be covered by my insurance. But other people with cars seemed to lend them out all the time, so I felt bad saying no, like I was being unreasonable and miserly if I didn't lend people my car. Gas was also very expensive, and I was conscious of other people riding with me all the time and not giving me gas money. Having a job helped minimize these feelings because money wasn't so tight.

I had an okay college soccer career but was not as successful as I had been previously. I had anterior cruciate ligament surgery my senior year in high school, then four more operations on the same knee by the time I graduated. This was likely part of the problem, but either way I did not have the personal success I had previously and was no longer the best player on the team. I was selected captain by my teammates, a role I held for three straight seasons, and I played and started in every game after my first season, so I still held an important leadership role on the team but was never one of the best players like I had always been in the past. The team was very successful. We played in the final four rounds of two national collegiate finals and lost in the quarter final a third year, and were consistently ranked in the top 10 teams in the country. As the captain of a top 10 team I felt a greater sense of responsibility for the team's success even if I wasn't one of the dominating players.

I did fine in school but never applied myself significantly; soccer was still my primary focus and academics came second. I finished with about a B plus average but no special honors or strong relationships with professors. It may have been partially because I was worried about trying really hard and still not being as successful as my fellow students. So I devoted more of my time and energy to the thing I thought I could excel at

Flash forward seven years: After working in the scrappy world of startup information technology–based firms where I often worked for little or no money and no benefits, I decided to go to business school. I haven't started yet, but going through the orientation and information sessions I have met many of my fellow students. Most come from finance or consulting backgrounds where they have made a lot of money. I feel more social pressure to have nice clothes, go out to nice dinners, buy drinks, go to shows, go to the Hamptons on weekends, and compare material things and elaborate trips. In this setting, probably more than any other, people seem to calculate status based on money, how much you have, how much you make—that's just how the cutthroat finance world seems to work. This feels a little different than it did during undergraduate school because money is more personal, whereas before it was more about what your parents had. I feel the social pressure to spend money more than I did before. I am also taking about $85K in loans to pay for school because I don't have a company paying for it. My parents have helped with small back-to-school gifts, and my aunt and uncle have given me $5K to help pay for school, but for the first time in my life I'm going into significant debt.

## Reflection question

Write a personal classnography, a personal narrative of your life from a social class perspective, and look at how your story is different from, or similar to, the stories of these real people.

## Discussion questions

Which of these stories or which part of one of these stories was like your life?

Were these stories different from the experiences of Whitney Page, Louise, Misty, Ursula, and Eleanor?

# CHAPTER 16

# *What Can Anyone Do?*

Class must be examined from multiple perspectives. Class is money, class is wealth, class is culture, class is prestige, class is education, class is occupation, and on and on. Underlying all this is the idea that class is personal. You create class every day, I create class every day. No abstract force is at work creating class. Only people create class. When you see a chair, a painting, a purse, or a pair of shoes and identify it as high prestige, then you have added class to the meaning of that chair, that painting, that purse, or that pair of shoes. When you meet Whitney Page or Louise and mentally assign her to a class, you have added class to the world. Class was not present until you added it. The creation of class gives advantages to some people and disadvantages to others.

Awareness, knowledge, and skill (Pope, Reynolds, & Mueller, 2004) are the big three when working with diversity. These concepts underlie everything in this chapter. Your awareness of class affects how you see problems and how you see solutions. If you believe that class is money and wealth, you will act on that view of class, you will see class issues as money and wealth issues, you will see money and wealth issues as class issues, and you will solve class problems as if they were money and wealth problems. If you believe class is cultural and social capital or education or prestige or occupation, you will act on that view of class.

"Those poor people just need to earn more money."

"Louise has such lower-class taste and manners. She needs to learn etiquette."

"Those people like Louise and Whitney Page just need to get more access to education."

And so on.

## Things you can do about class

Each chapter in this book contains enough content to make you more aware of social class so you can do something about the inequities of class. Managing, learning, and coming to terms with what we know, believe, and value is hard work. It is also basic work before beginning to engage others and your campus with class issues.

## Things you can encourage others on your campus to do about class

The idea that class is personal leads to the notion that the things to do about class are personal. Organizations, like colleges, are a collection of people, and you can effect change by structural, procedural, and interpersonal adjustments to the way your campus works.

*Conduct a campus class audit.* What are the policies and practices on your campus and how are these related to class, ethnicity, and gender? How do the policies and practices systematically give an advantage to one group and a disadvantage to another? Look at the time and money requirements for engagement, membership, and leadership. Catalog who is being served in your campus leadership workshops. Examine retention in terms of gender, ethnicity, and class.

The following are some examples of campus activities that put students from the underclass at a disadvantage:

♦ Move-in day on Friday with family orientation on Saturday assumes that at least one parent can get Friday off from work, and that the family can afford a hotel to stay for the Saturday orientation.

♦ Costs for attending events, memberships in organizations, concert and athletic tickets, alternative spring break, and even etiquette dinners are a part of every campus. Passing costs on to students is not always a good idea in that only some students can afford to pay these costs.

♦ Leadership development workshops may be for students who are already leaders. The criteria for attending should be examined.

Shared experiences and shared meanings are part of the core of shared culture. Class can be seen as a culture, and shared experiences and meanings become part of the social dialogue among community members. When a history professor comments on an army marching through the Arc de Triomphe, students who know about or who have been to Paris have an advantage in the ensuing class discussion. Using locations and experiences is part of the interaction process on campus, and the assumption of shared experiences reinforces the worldview that all normal people know about and have been to Europe, Hawaii, and other prestige destinations.

*Identify critical skills and knowledge.* What is the skill set and knowledge base that every one of your students needs to become academically and socially successful on your campus and after each one graduates? What academic class or student support service teaches these to all first-year students? A basic skills toolbox for all students certainly includes study, note taking, reading, writing, research, financial, technology, public speaking, quantitative, qualitative, modern, postmodern, and interpersonal skills. This is not a master list. Writers like Coplin (2003) identified 10 things employers want you to learn in college, and there are numerous lists of other skills that students need to be successful. Many of these skills, for example, oral and written communication in a work setting, require practice.

Do your campus administrators assume that all students come to campus with this skill toolbox, or do they assume that the better (read higher social class students) come to campus with this skill toolbox and that other students (read lower social class students) will pick it up? Do your campus administrators have a list of what should go in the skill toolbox? Note that this skill set is part of academic capital. Some colleges have a clear mission about helping students develop academic skills and a clear and articulated statement about these skills that is based on values and on research. Administrators at most campuses give students a tour of the library and throw everyone into the deep end of the pool, failing to realize that only the wealthier students had swimming lessons.

*Build a better bridge program.* This is a suggestion for every campus. Oddly, many of the program planners on the highly selective campuses have done this and put up first-year preceptorships to teach a specific skill set to all students. The idea of first-year experiences is old, going back to the first colleges in the United States. What is taught in those first-year experiences should be under continual examination and should center on the academic skill set all students need to be successful. First-year classes that focus solely on campus traditions (read cultural capital) at the expense of academic skills (read academic capital) should lose their funding.

Building a bridge program is a complex thing; balancing cultural capital with academic capital is a campus-specific process. Balancing the need for academic courses with the need to build academic skills for everyone is a complex campus-specific process. Helping all students understand the cultural capital of the class cultures around them without marginalizing the social class capital of the underclass is not easy. Creating events and activities for all class groups, especially with limited resources, is a political tightrope. These events should range from art openings to poetry slams, from etiquette dinners to country music festivals, from mock job interviews to exploring how to use college and explaining the campus financial aid systems. Identify people on campus who can articulate the cultural capital of different groups and use them as resources.

Bridge programs provide shared experiences and shared meaning for students, and these are part of the core of shared culture. Class can be seen as a culture, and the shared experiences and meanings become part of the social dialogue among community members. Creating a shared experience in study, social, critical thinking, and other skills you find necessary to be successful on your campus provides common ground for students to meet and cross gender, ethnicity, and class boundaries.

*Create awareness of class through campus programming.* Minority class students encounter class every day on campus. Whitney Page and Louise are aware of social class on campus every day because they see the markers of class above them and the structures and processes that exclude them. Ursula and Eleanor are aware of social class on campus every day because they see the markers of class below them and above them. The majority class student needs help in moving beyond denial, defense, and minimization toward acceptance, adaptation, and integration (Bennett, 1998). Creating events that will help majority students encounter and become aware of class is the only starting point that matters for them.

I am indebted to Dan Stoker and Carey Treager-Huber for their help with this chapter, so they get credit for the good stuff.

# References

Alger, H. (2010). *Luck and pluck*. New York: NY: Nabu Press. (Original work published 1869)

Alimo, C., Washington, J., & MacDonald-Dennis, C. (2003, March). *Beyond Secret Santa: Exploring Christian privilege*. Preconference workshop at the annual meeting of the American College Personnel Association, Minneapolis, MN.

Allen, W. (Director). (1983). *Zelig* [Motion picture]. USA: MGM.

American Psychological Association. (2009). *Publication Manual of the American Psychological Association* (6th ed.). Washington, DC: Author.

Astin, A. W. (1993). An empirical typology of college students. *Journal of College Student Development, 34*, 36–46.

Bandura, A. (1982). The psychology of chance encounters and life paths. *American Psychologist, 37*(7), 747–755.

Barratt, W. (2005). *Socioeconomic status: The inequitable campus*. Paper presented at the annual meeting of the American College Personnel Association, Nashville, TN.

Baxter-Magolda, M. B. (2009). *Authoring your life: Developing an internal voice to navigate life changes*. Sterling, VA: Stylus.

Bennett, M. (1998). Intercultural communication: A current perspective. In M. Bennett (Ed.), *Basic concepts of intercultural communication* (pp. 1–34). Boston, MA: Intercultural Press.

Berger, J. B. (2000). Oprimizing capital, social reproduction, and undergraduate persistence: A sociological perspective. In J. M. Braxton, (Ed.) *Reworking the student departure puzzle* (pp. 95–124). Nashville, TN: Vanderbilt University Press.

Blumer, H. (1969). *Symbolic interactionism: Perspective and method*. Berkeley, CA: University of California Press.

Bolman, L. G., & Deal, T. E. (2008). *Reframing organizations: Artistry, choice, and leadership.* San Francisco, CA: Jossey-Bass.

Bourdieu, P. (1986). The forms of capital. In J. Richardson (Ed.), *Handbook of theory and research for the sociology of education* (pp. 241–258). New York, NY: Greenwood Press.

boyd, d. (2007). *Viewing American class divisions through Facebook and My-Space.* Retrieved March 4, 2008, from http://www.danah.org/papers/essays/ClassDivisions.html

Boyer, E. (1988). *College: The undergraduate experience in America.* New York, NY: HarperCollins.

Bradburn, D., Hurst, D., & Peng, S. (2001). *Community college transfer rates to 4-year institutions using alternative definitions of transfer.* Washington, DC: U.S. Department of Education.

Brill, S. (Director). (2002). *Mr. Deeds.* [Motion picture] USA: Columbia Pictures.

Brooks, M. (Director). (1981). *History of the world: Part I* [Motion picture]. USA: Brooksfilms.

Carey, K. (2006) *College rankings reformed.* Washington, DC: Education Sector.

Cataldi, E. F., Laird, J., KewalRamani, A., & Chapman, C. (2009). *High school dropout and completion rates in the United States: 2007.* Washington, DC: National Center for Education Statistics.

Chickering, A. W. (1972). *Education and identity.* San Francisco, CA: Jossey-Bass.

Chickering, A. W., & Reisser, L. (1983). *Education and identity.* San Francisco, CA: Jossey-Bass.

Cline, C. (n.d.). *Payday.* Retrieved from http://www.steamiron.com/payday

Coplin, W. D. (2003). *10 things employers want you to learn in college: The know-how you need to succeed.* Berkeley, CA: Ten Speed Press.

Cross, W. (1978). The Thomas and Cross models of psychological Nigrescence: A review. *Journal of Black Psychology, 5,* 13–21.

Cross, W. (1991). *Shades of Black: Diversity in African-American identity.* Philadelphia, PA: Temple University Press.

Cross, W. E. (1995). The psychology of Nigrescence: Revising the Cross model. In J. G. Ponterotto, J. M. Casas, L. A. Suzuki, & C. M. Alexander (Eds.), *Handbook of multicultural counseling* (pp. 93–122). Thousand Oaks, CA: Sage.

Cukor, G. (Director). (1964). *My fair lady* [Motion picture]. USA: Warner Brothers.

Davis, J., Smith, T., Hodge, R., Nakao, K., & Treas, J. (1991). *Occupational prestige ratings from the 1989 general social survey.* Ann Arbor, MI: Inter-university Consortium for Political and Social Research.

DeCosta, M. (1958). *Auntie Mame* [Motion picture]. USA: Warner Brothers.

Dews, C. L., & Law, C. L. (1995). *This fine place so far from home: Voices of academics from the working class.* Philadelphia, PA: Temple University Press.

Doyle, A. C. (1887). *A study in scarlet.* London: Ward Lock & Co.

Educational Testing Service. (2007). *2007 College-bound seniors national report.* Princeton, NJ: Author.

Eliscu, J. (2005). *Schools that rock: The* Rolling Stone *college guide.* New York, NY: Wenner.

Erikson, E. (1968). *Identity: Youth and crisis.* New York, NY: Norton.

Evans, N. J., Forney, D. S., Guido, F. M., Patton, L. D., & Renn, K. A. (2010). *Student development in college: Theory, research, and practice.* San Francisco, CA: Jossey-Bass.

Falk, G. (2001). *Stigma: How we treat outsiders.* New York, NY: Prometheus Books.

Feldman, K. A., & Newcomb, T. M. (1969). *The impact of college on students: Volume 1.* San Francisco, CA: Jossey-Bass.

Fitzgerald, F. S. (2005). *The rich boy.* London, UK: Hesperus Press.

Frankel, D. (Director). (2006). *The devil wears Prada* [Motion picture]. USA: 20th Century Fox.

Granfield, R. (1991). Making it by faking it: Working-class students in an elite academic environment. *Journal of Contemporary Ethnography, 20,* 331–351.

Goffman, E. (1959). *The presentation of self in everyday life.* New York, NY: Anchor Books.

Haggis, P. (Director). (2004). *Crash* [Motion picture]. USA: Lions Gate Films.

Helms, J. E. (1995). An update of Helms's White and people of color racial identity models. In J. M. Casas, L. A. Suzuki, & C. M. Alexander (Eds.), *Handbook of multicultural counseling* (pp. 181–189). Thousand Oaks, CA: Sage.

Hess, S. (2007). *Navigating class on campus: The peer culture of working class undergraduates.* Unpublished doctoral dissertation, Boston College, Boston, MA.

Hofstadter, R. (1963). *Anti-intellectualism in American life.* New York, NY: Knopf.

Hofstede, G., & Hofstede, G. J. (2006). *Cultures and organizations: Software of the mind.* New York, NY: McGraw-Hill.

Holland, J. (1973). *Making vocational choices: A theory of careers.* Englewood Cliffs, NJ: Prentice-Hall.

Hollingshead, A. B. (1957). *Two factor index of social position.* New Haven, CT: Unpublished manuscript. Department of Sociology, Yale University.

Hollingshead, A. B. (1975). *Four factor index of social status.* Unpublished manuscript, Yale University, New Haven, CT.

hooks, b. (2000). *Where we stand: Class matters.* New York, NY: Routledge.

Ishitani, T. (2006). Studying attrition and degree completion behavior among first-generation college students in the United States. *The Journal of Higher Education, 77*(5), 861–885.

Josselson, R. (1987). *Finding herself: Pathways to identity development in women.* San Francisco, CA: Jossey-Bass.

Kaufman, P. (2003). Learning to not labor: How working-class individuals construct middle-class identities. *Sociological Quarterly, 44,* 481–504.

Kouzes, J. M., & Posner, B. Z. (2003). *Credibility: How leaders gain and lose it, why people demand it.* San Francisco, CA: Jossey-Bass.

Kramer, S. (Director). (1967). *Guess who's coming to dinner?* [Motion picture] USA: Columbia Pictures.

La Cava, G. (Director). (1936). *My man Godfrey* [Motion picture]. USA: Columbia Pictures.

LaFromboise, T., Coleman, H. L., & Gerton, J. (1993). Psychological impact of biculturalism: Evidence and theory. *Psychological Bulletin, 114,* 395–412.

Landis, J. (Director). (1991). *Oscar* [Motion picture]. USA: Walt Disney Video.

Levitt, S., & Dubner, S. (2006). *Freakonomics: A rogue economist explores the hidden side of everything.* New York, NY: William Morrow.

Luhrmann, B. (Director). (1996). *Romeo + Juliet* [Motion picture]. USA: Bazmark Films.

Marcia, J. (1966). Development and validation of ego-identity status. *Journal of Personality and Social Psychology, 5,* 551–558.

Marcia, J. (1967). Ego identity status: Relationship to change in self-esteem, "general maladjustment," and authoritarianism. *Journal of Personality, 35,* 118–133.

Marcia, J. (1994). The empirical study of ego identity. In H. Bosma, D. De Levita, & H. brotevant, (Eds.), *Identity and development: An interdisciplinary approach* (pp. 67–80). Thousand Oaks, CA: Sage.

Marshall, G. (Director). (1990). *Pretty woman* [Motion picture]. USA: Touchstone Pictures.

Marx, K. (1906). *Capital: A critique of political economy.* New York, NY: Modern Library.

Marx, K., & Engels, F. (1954). *The communist manifesto* (S. Moore, Trans.). Chicago, IL: Henry Regnery. Original work published 1848

McEwen. (2003). New perspectives on identity development. In S. Komives, D. Woodard Jr., & Associates (Eds.), *Student services: A handbook for the profession* (pp. 203–233). San Francisco, CA: Jossey-Bass.

McIntosh, P. (1988). *Unpacking the invisible knapsack.* Wellesley, MA: Wellesley College Center for Research on Women.

Moos, R. (1974). *Issues in social ecology: Human milieus.* New York, NY: National Press Books.

National Center for Education Statistics. (1998) *First generation students: Undergraduates whose parents never enrolled in post-secondary education.* Retrieved from http://nces.edu.gov/pubs98/98082.pdf

National Center for Education Statistics. (2005). *First-generation students in postsecondary education: A look at their college transcripts.* Washington, DC: U.S. Department of Education.

National Study of Student Engagement. (2000). *The NSSE 2000 report: National benchmarks of effective educational practice.* Bloomington, IN: Author.

Nelson, M. L., Englar-Carlson, M., Tierney, S. C., & Hau, J. M. (2006). Class jumping into academia: Multiple identities for counseling academics. *Journal of Counseling Psychology, 53*(1), 1–14.

*New York Times.* (2005). *Class matters.* Retrieved from http://www.nytimes.com/packages/html/national/20050515_CLASS_GRAPHIC/index_01.html

Nunez, A., & Cuccaro-Alamin, S. (1998). *First-generation students: Undergraduates whose parents never enrolled in postsecondary education* (NCES Report 98-082). Washington, DC: U.S. Department of Education, National Center for Education Statistics. Retrieved from http://nces.ed.gov/pubs98/98082.pdf

Orwell, G. (1949). *1984.* New York, NY: Signet Classics.

Pascarella, E. T., Pierson, C. T., Wolniak, G. C., & Terenzini, P. T. (2004). First-generation college students: Additional evidence on college experiences and outcomes. *Journal of Higher Education, 75,* 249–284.

Pascarella, E., & Terenzini, P. (2005). *How college affects students: A third decade of research* (Vol. 2). San Francisco, CA: Wiley.

Pascarella, E. T., & Terenzini, P. T. (1991). *How college affects students: Findings and insights from twenty years of research.* San Francisco, CA: Jossey-Bass.

Pascarella, E. T., Wolniak, G., Pierson, C., & Terenzini, P. (2003). Experiences and outcomes of first-generation students in community colleges. *Journal of College Student Development, 44*, 420–429.

Pope, L. (2000). *Colleges that change lives: 40 schools you should know about even if you are not a straight-A student.* New York, NY: Penguin.

Pope, L. R., Reynolds, A. L., & Mueller, J. A. (2004). *Multicultural competence in student affairs.* San Francisco, CA: Jossey-Bass.

Rest, J. (1979) *Development in judging moral issues.* Minneapolis, MN: University of Minnesota Press.

Rosenbaum, J. (1972). *Is your Volkswagen a sex symbol?* Portland, OR: Hawthorn Books.

Sacks, P. (2007). *Tearing down the gates: Confronting the class divide in American education.* Los Angeles, CA: University of California Press.

Schwartz, S. (Producer). (1964–1967). *Gilligan's island* [Television series]. Hollywood, CA: Columbia Broadcasting System.

Singer, B. (Director). (1995). *The usual suspects* [Motion picture]. USA: MGM.

Stevens, M. L. (2007). *Creating a class: College admissions and the education of elites.* Cambridge, MA: Harvard University Press.

Strange, C., & Banning, J. (2001). *Educating by design.* San Francisco, CA: Jossey-Bass.

Stuber, J. M. (2005). Talk of class: The discursive repertoires of White working- and upper-middle-class college students. *Journal of Contemporary Ethnography, 35*, 285–318.

Tan, A. (1989). *The joy luck club.* New York, NY: Ivy Books.

Terenzini, P. T., Springer, L., Yaeger, P. M., Pascarella, E. T., & Nora, A. (1996). First generation college students: Characteristics, experiences, and cognitive development. *Research in Higher Education, 37*(1), 1–22.

Tinto, V. (1993). *Leaving college: Rethinking the causes and cures of student attrition.* Chicago, IL: University of Chicago Press.

Torres, V., Howard-Hamilton, M., & Cooper, D. L. (2002). *Identity development of diverse populations: Implications for teaching and administration in higher education.* San Francisco, CA: Jossey-Bass.

Twain, M. (1981). *The adventures of Tom Sawyer.* New York, NY: Bantam Classic. (Original work published 1875)

U.S. Census Bureau. (2007). *Educational attainment in the United States: 2007.* Retrieved from http://www.census.gov/prod/2009pubs/p20=560.pdf

U.S. Census Bureau. (2008a). *Educational attainment in the United States: 2008—Detailed tables. Table 1, all races.* Retrieved from http://www.census.gov/hhes/socdemo/education/data/cps/2009/tables.html

U.S. Census Bureau. (2008b). *Income: Households, Table H-1. Income limits for each fifth and top 5 percent, all races.* Retrieved from http://www.census .gov/hhes/www/income/data/historical/household/index.html

U.S. Census Bureau. (2009). *Table 705. Family net worth—mean and median net worth in constant (2007) dollars by selected family characteristics: 1998– 2007.* Retrieved from http://www.census.gov/compendia/statab/tables/ 08s0699.pdf

U.S. Department of Education. (2006). *A test of leadership: Charting the future of U.S. Higher education.* Washington, DC: U.S. Department of Education.

Van Galen, J. (2000). Education & class. *Multicultural Education, 7*(3), 2–11.

Ward, D. (Director). (1982). *Cannery row* [Motion picture] . USA: MGM.

White, L. (1949). *The science of culture.* New York, NY: Grove Press.

X, M. (1965). *Autobiography of Malcom X.* New York: Castle Books.

Zemsky, R. (2007, January 26). The rise and fall of the Spellings Commission. *Chronicle Review,* p. B6.

Zweig, M. (2000). *The working class majority: America's best kept secret.* Ithaca, NY: Cornell University Press.

# Index

# Textbooks from Stylus

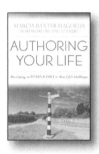

### Authoring Your Life
*Developing an Internal Voice to Navigate Life's Challenges*
Marcia B. Baxter Magolda
Illustrated by Matthew Henry Hall
Foreword by Sharon Daloz Parks

"No one has carried the concept of 'self-authorship' forward more richly, or with greater use for the reader, than Marcia Baxter Magolda. Anyone interested in supporting their own, or others', adult development will benefit enormously from this book."—*Robert Kegan*, *Meehan Professor of Adult Learning, Harvard University, and co-author of "Immunity to Change"*

But this is not simply a self-help book. We live in a time when we need more grown-ups. We need citizens who do not just 'go with the flow' and who can think for themselves about the questions of not only our individual lives but also the changing life of our society, our world, our planet."—*Sharon Daloz Parks*, author of *"Big Questions, Worthy Dreams: Mentoring Young Adults in Their Search for Meaning, Purpose and Faith"*; and *"Leadership Can Be Taught: A Bold Approach for a Complex World"*

### We ARE Americans
*Undocumented Students Pursuing the American Dream*
William Perez
Foreword by Daniel G. Solorzano

"This fascinating look at the next generation of undocumented immigrants unpacks the complexities of the debate and puts unforgettable human faces to its subjects. Perez, a developmental psychologist and professor in Southern California, plumbs the stories of students living with the constant threat of deportation for an answer to the question, 'What does it mean to be an American?'"—*Publishers Weekly*, *Starred Web Pick of the Week*

"In-depth description and numerous quotes from Perez's interviews make this book a useful resource for students and scholars of immigration and education, as well as for general readers looking for first-person stories of immigration."—*Library Journal*

### Multiculturalism on Campus
*Theory, Models, and Practices for Understanding Diversity and Creating Inclusion*
Edited by Michael Cuyjet, Mary F. Howard-Hamilton, and Diane L. Cooper

"*Multiculturalism on Campus* is a *tour de force*. In this single volume noted scholars have created an excellent textbook for undergraduate and graduate students; a teaching tool for faculty; and, a comprehensive resource for all who strive for multiculturalism and social justice on college campuses." —*Paul Shang*, *Assistant Vice President and Dean of Students, University of Oregon, Past President, ACPA-College Student Educators International*

22883 Quicksilver Drive
Sterling, VA 20166-2102          Subscribe to our e-mail alerts: www.Styluspub.com